Neil Prem is a sought-after change-makers and entre their gift and do what me has a gift and message that the world desperately needs, and he shows you how to start where you are, use what you have and do what you can.

Polly Gilbert, co-founder of TAP London, says he's 'a start-up genius' and serial entrepreneur David Thomson calls him 'the most profound and insightful person I have ever known'.

Neil has helped over 1500 change-makers from 50 nations to live on purpose and become thought leaders who people want to follow, and to create hundreds of new social ventures, businesses and community projects.

He has written for *The Coach* and *Liberty* magazine, has been interviewed by the BBC and has led workshops at some of the world's leading universities, including Oxford and Cambridge.

Neil was one of the first professional coaches in the UK, has personally trained over 40 career coaches and has developed the widely used 12 Core Dynamics, iCARE and DREAM coaching models. He also co-founded the Allia Serious Impact Programme.

Neil is a stroke survivor, has lived, worked and travelled in over 25 nations and loves street art, cricket and coffee.

You can connect with and follow him at:

w: neilprem.com

e: neil@neilprem.com

t: @neilprem

This book is dedicated to the following people:

Esther Prem: for always being there for me over the last 30 years.

Hannah and Lydia Prem: sorry about Father Christmas.

Alan and Meg Prem: you dared to be different and followed your dreams.

June Harvey: the most fearless woman I have ever known – a true inspiration.

Jayne Keady: you made me feel safe when the world didn't.

This is a work of creative non-fiction. Some parts have been fictionalised in varying degrees for various purposes. Every effort has been made to trace or contact all copyright holders. The publishers will be pleased to make good any omissions or rectify any mistakes brought to their attention at the earliest opportunity.

Printed in the United Kingdom
First paperback edition 2019

Book design by Vanessa Mendozzi

ISBN: 9781076343109 (paperback)

Routes Publishing
www.routesuk.com

7 Steps *to* PURPOSE

HOW TO GET UNSTUCK, DISCOVER YOUR GIFT AND DO WHAT MATTERS MOST

NEIL PREM

Acknowledgements

With special thanks to:

All of my beautiful, brilliant and exceptionally fearless friends, family and clients for supporting me.

Caroline Hyde, Paul Hughes, Ania Karbownik and all of the really nice people at Allia Ltd for giving me the time, space and resources to explore my ideas and convictions.

Dhanya Gokul for her help with the design and branding for Routes.

Julia Kellaway for brilliant editing.

Vanessa Mendozzi for her wonderful typesetting and cover design.

Contents

Introduction   1

PART 1 - WHERE NOW, WHAT NEXT?   9

Chapter 1 - The Abundant Life   11

Chapter 2 - Turning Points   25

Chapter 3 - Disconnected   45

Chapter 4 - Alignment   59

PART 2 - SEVEN STEPS TO PURPOSE   77

Chapter 5 - Step 1: Slow Down   79

Chapter 6 - Step 2: Get Out of Your Head   95

Chapter 7 - Step 3: Remember Who You Are   111

Chapter 8 - Step 4: Let Go of the Past   135

Chapter 9 - Step 5: Find Your Why   155

Chapter 10 - Step 6: Discover Your Gift   169

Chapter 11 - Step 7: Find Your Flow   187

Chapter 12 - Take Action   205

Conclusion   221

Note from the Author: Ordinary Superheroes Wanted   233

Testimonials   235

INTRODUCTION

There is a life available to us – a life of meaning and purpose, connection and contribution; a life of joy and peace and effortless flow. We all want that life and we're searching for it each and every day. However, though we search for it, and occasionally experience it, we never truly live it.

We're so busy running around feeling stressed and anxious all the time, desperately trying to be more and do more so that we can ultimately have more, that we never have the time to realise that there is a better way to live and experience life. All of this running around means that we often find ourselves at a crossroads looking for a better way.

At these times we feel stuck and confused and don't know what to do. If we do have a sense of what we need to do, we often find ourselves lacking the courage to make it happen. We feel plagued by fear and insecurity.

This doubt and confusion are messages letting us know that change needs to happen. Messages from deep within, quietly informing us that something is wrong and that we can't keep going on living this way – we need to do something different. However, we're often so desperate to move on and avoid the pain and discomfort that we never fully hear or receive these messages.

The reason we're experiencing this doubt and confusion is that we're disconnected and misaligned. There is a disconnection between what we really want and what we believe is possible and there is a misalignment between the work we're doing on a daily basis and the work that we're meant to do. We're headed down the wrong path.

With the passing of time, and with the benefit of hindsight, we eventually discover that these crossroads were in fact turning points; opportunities when life itself tapped us on the shoulder to let us know that there was a better way, when we were presented with an invitation to realign in order for change to happen.

Before we can effectively realign, we need to create space in order for change to happen. We need to learn to slow down, breathe and get out of our heads. We need to do less, and, as you'll come to see, the paradox is that often the less we do, the more we get done.

Having created space in order for change to happen, we then simply need to do three things to effortlessly allow for that change to happen:

Reconnect

We need to reconnect to our gifts, calling and true identity, to see ourselves for who we really are and to (re)connect to infinite possibilities.

Let go of the past

We need to let go of the lies we've believed about ourselves, the world and our place in it. We need to let go of the past with all of its pain and regret. We need to learn to forgive and forget.

Take inspired action

We need to engage in a meaningful and intentional act of contribution, to help somebody else. We need to intentionally bring more of our true nature (our gifts, talents and passion) to what we do. Growth and giving to others will guide us back home.

If we don't listen and respond to the messages that life is bringing us, we will find ourselves at another crossroads. Whether that's in months or years to come, we will eventually find ourselves stuck, once again, feeling lost and confused with even less idea about what to do next. The challenge is that at each subsequent crossroads we experience greater levels of doubt and confusion. This book will help you to move forward successfully and with purpose.

If we hear and respond to the messages that our pain and discomfort are bringing us, and shift from disconnection to alignment, we will really begin to experience the abundant life that we're meant to live and that is freely available to us.

As we remember who we really are and connect to infinite possibilities we'll feel confident to do what it takes to follow our dreams. We'll let go of the lies we've believed about ourselves, the world and our place in it, and we'll finally become the person we were born to be – bold, uncaged and free. When we align who we are with what we do and learn to keep taking inspired action we'll finally say yes to our calling and do the work we're meant to do. We'll live with incredible meaning and purpose. We'll make the contribution that we're here to make and we'll step into effortless flow.

This is a life worth living and this book was written to inspire you to do just that.

Who This Book is For

This book is for those who long to bring their gifts and

message to the world and make their own special contribution. It's for those who want to find and claim their unique place, but something is holding them back. This book is for people who are spiritual but not necessarily religious. This book is a map for those who know and recognise that something needs to change in order for that to happen and are ready to make that change – albeit nervously.

If you're reading this, I want you to know that I believe in you. You have gifts and talents that your companies, organisations and communities desperately need.

When I look at you, I see someone who is not a mistake and who is here for a reason. I see someone who is fearfully and wonderfully made. I see someone with a talent and message that the world desperately needs. I love that your flaws, imperfections and mistakes are a part of your unique story; your message. I see someone who can create anything they put their mind to. I see someone who has within them the power to make all of their dreams, ideas and callings a wonderful living reality. I see someone ready to take the next step.

You see something in the world that has to change and are in touch with what needs to change. You have ideas and the passion to do something about it and are ready for someone to see that potential in you, come alongside you and provide you with the space and encouragement to begin your journey of transformation – to become the person you were born to be, to do the work you are meant to do and to live the life you're meant to live. This is your time.

Your passion is the God-given desire to invest your time, talent and energy in what matters most. The world needs your passion.

My hope is that you will awaken to your true potential; that you will sense a call to step into your purpose. Whatever your dreams, I want to help you make them happen. No matter how big or small, if it's important to you then it's important to me and to the world.

My Promise

If you listen to the message life is bringing to you and begin to align with it, you will start to fully awaken to your gifts and talents, uncover your unique message and go boldly out into the world sharing what God has so freely given you to the benefit of others. It will lead to a level of personal freedom, connection and contribution.

It will lead to change. That might include wanting to change career or starting an inspired business that works for so much more than profit. It might lead to you to investing a few hours a week to start a community project that transforms the lives of people and communities. It will take you on a journey of infinite possibilities.

My dream is to see an army – a global force for good – awakened to their true potential. Let go of any fear and insecurity and begin to fly. If just one person does this, I will consider this book a success.

Our deepest fear is not that we are inadequate. Our deepest fear is that we are powerful beyond measure. It is our light, not our darkness that most frightens us. We ask ourselves, Who am I to be brilliant, gorgeous, talented, fabulous? Actually, who are you not to be? You are a child of God. Your playing small does not serve the world. There is nothing enlightened about shrinking so that other people won't feel insecure around you. We are all meant to shine, as children do. We were born to make manifest the glory of God that is within us. It's not just in some of us; it's in everyone. And as we let our own light shine, we unconsciously give other people permission to do the same. As we are liberated from our own fear, our presence automatically liberates others.

Marianne Williamson, *A Return to Love*

PART 1

Where Now, What Next?

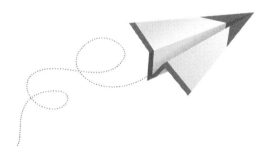

CHAPTER 1

The Abundant Life

There is this life, which I call the abundant life, which we all want to live and experience. It's a life of meaning, purpose, connection and contribution, adventure, personal growth, happiness and unlimited success. It's a life free from worry and anxiety.

If proof were needed, you only need to search online for 'passion' and you'll find some 1.6 billion pages offering thoughts and advice on the subject. If you search for 'life purpose' you'll find over 5 billion pages, and if you search for 'calling' you'll return a staggering 9.5 billion pages to visit and explore. On YouTube you can watch Adam Leipzig's talk – 'How to know your life purpose in 5 minutes' – which has over 13 million views. One of the most popular books on the subject of abundant living – Rick Warren's *The Purpose Driven Life* – has sold over 34 million copies.

Most of us want much more from life. We want to wake up each day and know where we're going and that we're on track to get there. We want to experience profound joy and happiness and deep connection with others. We want all this and are desperately striving to take hold of it, but it always seems to be just out of reach.

The abundant life is the life we're meant to live. We do not have to strive to attain it and it's available to everybody. There is enough joy, happiness and resources for everyone to have all that they want and desire. Nobody gets left out or left behind. When we experience the abundant life, our natural state is one of joy, peace and happiness, free from all stress and anxiety. It's a life of effortless creative flow, where everything is realised through deliberate intention. It's a life where we live fully supported; where God has our back and we feel His contagious pleasure in all that we say and do. It's a life where everything is possible, and nothing is impossible. No matter how big, small or crazy our dreams are, every one of them has already been stamped with 'Approved', and the circumstances we need to make them happen are already conspiring in our favour. All we have to do is rest, secure in the knowledge that all things are working for our benefit at all times.

This book, and the seven steps it offers, will provide you with a roadmap to the abundant life. No matter how difficult your present situation or how painful your past, you can find and enjoy an abundant life. We'll explore stories of people who found it and how they got there, and you'll see that you can have it too. Let's begin by looking at what makes up an abundant life.

Meaning and Purpose

There is a story that I suspect is one of those urban legends that isn't actually true, but we want it to be true because it has a deep ring of truth about it and speaks directly to us. This story is about Sir Christopher Wren, the architect for St Paul's Cathedral, completed in 1710.

The story says that Sir Christopher was making a site visit to see the progress being made at St Paul's and, as he toured the site, his eyes couldn't help being drawn to three bricklayers working a short distance from him. He noted that the difference in their attitude and energy was really quite staggering. The first was slow and cumbersome; he clearly didn't want to put in any more effort than he had to. The second was working at a steady pace but there was no joy in his eyes. The third was working furiously while singing hymns at the top of his voice.

Sir Christopher stared at them for a few minutes before his curiosity got the better of him, and he wandered over to engage with the men. 'What are you three working on?' he cheerfully asked.

'I'm laying bricks,' said the first.

'I'm building a wall,' said the second.

'I'm building a house for my God, where all men may come and enjoy Him,' declared the third.

We want to be like the last man, living each day connected to a story much bigger than ourselves.

Meaning and purpose is something we all want from our work and lives. To wake up each day with a sense that there is a purpose to what we're doing, a story unfolding behind the stresses and strains of each day. To know that what we're doing is important.

For many of us, myself included, we want to know that there is a much deeper spiritual meaning to our lives. We want to believe that there is a greater force at work in the universe and that a gentle loving hand is shaping our lives and destiny. We sense a call – a voice that speaks in such gentle tones, ever so quietly to us, particularly at night, when our eyes close but our ears continue to hear that voice and reflect it back in our dreams. We want to know that we are being connected to something much greater than ourselves.

Meaning and purpose are fully available to us when we experience the abundant life through connecting what we love, want and are meant to do, with what we actually do on a daily basis.

Contribution

We want to make a contribution to this world. There exists within each of us a deep desire to make a difference, to know that what we're doing and have done are somehow making a real, genuine and authentic contribution to the lives of others and the planet.

Happiness is found through contribution. Why else would we give so much to charity or willingly volunteer our time, talent and energy to help others? Why else would we sit glued to the TV watching *Children in Need?* Why do hundreds of people generously give their time and talents to help people less fortunate, in TV programmes such as *DIY SOS?*

When we help others, we experience a deep sense of joy and gratitude. We feel a genuine connection to those we serve and a continual desire to help more.

Our ability to make our personal contribution occurs when we use our unique gifts, talents and energy to serve others and help solve their problems. Using our gifts to serve others in the areas that matter most allows us to experience what can only be described as a deep sense of 'flow'– moments when we lose ourselves, lost in the moment when time stands still. This sense of flow is rarely found anywhere else – it's spiritual, possibly even divine and holy. It's a feeling that only comes when we know that we're doing the work that we're meant to do.

Spontaneity and Adventure

We want to live adventurously, and we crave variety, interest and spontaneity. We queue for hours to ride roller coasters and some of us will even travel thousands of miles to experience the biggest, tallest and scariest rides on the planet. We jump out of planes, raft down fast-flowing rivers and trek across baking hot deserts.

We are a species of thrill seekers, adventurers and innovators. Our need for variety and change allowed us to discover new continents, create art and music, cook with spices and change our clothes every season. We want spontaneity and yet we also want stability:

stability + variety = happiness

Stability and variety can be seen as different ends of the same spectrum with a fulcrum in the middle, like a seesaw. Swing too much in either direction and you'll immediately feel the need to rebalance. We want both stability and variety, and obtaining enough of both is the key: learning to flow with our own natural rhythm of enough stability and adventure, spontaneity and predictability, and understanding how long we can keep doing the same things and experiencing the same routines before we crave variety, change and adventure. The abundant life offers both.

We want to live our lives free from boredom and anxiety and free from the negative behaviours that take away the emotions that overwhelm us. We don't want to feel that our work is boring and repetitive. We don't want to feel that life is being lived on a conveyor belt.

Personal Growth

We want to be the best version of ourselves. We want to live up to our potential, to achieve all that we can and to live a life without regrets.

From the moment of conception, our human nature wants to grow, achieve and overcome. Even before the moment of conception, millions of sperm race against each other to fertilise the egg. Our DNA carries within it the desire to develop and grow.

The newborn baby will scream for food in order that she can grow. She learns to crawl in order to move towards what she wants. Once she can crawl, she'll want to walk and will persevere as she tumbles and falls, never giving up. She'll teach herself to speak so that she can better communicate her needs, wants and desires. And the story keeps going… The child follows her passions and learns new skills. She compares herself with others and in doing so wants to compete. She sets herself goals and trains herself to achieve all that she sets her mind towards. She fails and she learns and keeps going until she achieves her goals. She is happy with the stability her achievement brings and then seeks greater variety and then works to become more, do more and achieve more.

They say necessity is the mother of all invention. Behind that necessity, is the primal desire to continually improve, grow and achieve. The survival of the human race depends on it. It is fully human to want to build a bridge across a river, rather than wade across it.

The desire to become the best version of ourselves is also the desire to better understand ourselves, to grow in the knowledge of who we are, to establish our own identity and to increase our self-esteem. We want to learn and satisfy our curiosity. We want to know what happens when we mix two colours or chemicals together. We want to make intellectual connections – to understand how the world works and might work for our benefit.

Connection

We want to live connected lives. To journey through life with others, especially those who think and feel the same as us. To be seen, heard and celebrated by others is one of the greatest joys life can offer. To know and be known is one of the fundamental purposes of life.

Stephen Covey in his book *The 8th Habit* says that the purpose of life is to live, love, learn and leave a legacy. Of these, the greatest is love.

Some of the first words ever spoken confirmed what we now know – that it is not good for man to be alone. We are social creatures by nature. From cradle to grave we need and want to relate. We are born connected. Once the umbilical cord is cut, that connection is severed and we begin to seek it again and, once found, cherish it throughout our entire life.

Every baby naturally seeks to bond with its mother; his brain won't develop properly without him being held and he intuitively knows that his survival depends on it. The baby becomes a child and begins to intentionally seek out companions and friendships at school. The teenager finds a tribe to belong to and a best friend in whom he can confide, eventually becoming an adult who wants a life partner. Together they then want children and grandchildren. These families build communities with others and centre their lives around those communities and then, at the end of those lives, their children, family and friends grieve, often for years, at the passing of their parents. We function at our best in close proximity to others.

At every stage in life, we crave connection with others: family, friends, tribes, lovers and colleagues. Not only do we want to connect with others, we want others to love and connect with us. There is a deep and even fundamental desire in each person for the need to be seen, heard, valued and understood by others, and that only happens through relationships.

None of us wants to live alone and isolated from others. Psychologists study and understand the long-term effects of those starved of love and affection. It is now widely known that social isolation quickly leads to mental health issues. As the Beatles said, 'All you need is love, love. Love is all you need.'

Success

We want to succeed in life. We want to have goals and to see them happen. At its core, life is a journey of intention and action, deciding what we want and then pursuing it. Whether you call these goals dreams, desires or callings, the wonderful truth is that we get to choose what we want out of life and have the right to go after it. No one else has the right to tell us what we can and can't have – although many do.

Each of us builds a picture of the life we want for ourselves and our families, and we also have a picture of what we believe we deserve and is possible. We inherently understand that for our intentions to happen both pictures need to be the same.

Each of us has different ideas of what success looks like: for some it's determined monetarily, for others it's through their accomplishments, while for others it's related to being fit and healthy, their quality of life, the places they visit, the knowledge that they acquire, the friends that they make or the children they raise.

Some set seemingly impossible goals – to climb the highest mountains or to visit every country in the world, to fly in space, to run the fastest mile, to speak to multitudes or make millions of dollars. And yet every day we hear of people achieving their impossible goals, doing exactly what only a few years ago would have been thought of as impossible. When we're living the abundant life, nothing is impossible for us. We dare to dream and are not hindered in any way from setting our mind to whatever we want and can imagine.

Everyone is born with the desire to succeed, the capacity to determine what it is that they want from life and an inbuilt drive to pursue it fully. Many of us are not pursuing our own dreams. We're living somebody else's life and we wake up one day to discover, as Stephen Covey said, 'That the ladder we've been climbing is leaning up against the wrong wall.' Even at those times when we realise we've been heading in the wrong direction, we get to start again and decide what it is that we want in life and pursue it once more. We are only ever one intention away from transforming our current reality.

There is nothing quite like achieving a goal in life. The joy that comes from having worked towards something we want and achieving it is unparalleled.

Happiness

We want to be happy; to live and experience life in all its fullness. We want to enjoy our passions, follow our dreams and do the work that matters. We want to break away from the treadmill of searching but never finding.

Control

In his 2006 TED Talk, Tony Robbins said that one of the

top five needs of people is to be in control of their lives, which he translates as the need and desire for stability. We want control over our lives. When we have control, or at least the illusion of control, we feel at peace, are centred and calm.

We want stability from knowing that we are on the right path to get what we want and to know that we are taking the right steps to achieve our goals. We also want to know that we're making sufficient progress, that nothing will go wrong or that nothing unplanned will happen. In our minds, stability equals control.

When we're living on purpose, we realise that control is an illusion and we are quick to let go of the lie that we can control anything. What we do know is that we are loved and wanted and that, moment by moment, we are being taken care of, that everything we need will be there when we need it. We know that we lack nothing. We don't fear trouble and, if it should come, we know that everything will work out for our benefit in the end.

The Big Decision

Einstein said, 'I think the most important question facing humanity is, "Is the universe a friendly place?" This is the first and most basic question all people must answer for themselves.'

When we understand that the universe is friendly, very friendly indeed, we will then realise that the abundant life is freely available to us. All we have to do is ask, believe and receive. This is the life that we want and, when we learn to align our hearts – what we really want and desire – with our heads – what we believe we deserve and believe is possible – we can find it and experience it like never before.

As we'll see in the next chapter, life itself is regularly sending us a message, trying to get our attention. A message that speaks of our disconnection and our misalignment and why change needs to happen. A message that we desperately need but are struggling to hear.

CHAPTER 2

Turning Points

In our pursuit of the abundant life there are many times when we find ourselves at a crossroads looking for purpose and direction, asking ourselves where now and what next? These times can feel very lonely and confusing. The pain and confusion are signs that we are not living the life that we want and that is available to us.

We reach these crossroads because there is something missing in our lives, something we're subconsciously searching for. There's a part of us that is not being honoured and expressed. Whether that's a talent, a value, a calling or a deep interest, there is some part of us that gets left at home each day, doesn't come to work, isn't being expressed and needs a meaningful outlet.

Deep down we know this to be true. Our intuition reminds us that change must happen. We often know which part of us is crying out for expression but somehow that voice gets lost, drowned out by all the other voices demanding choices.

If we suppress that voice, it will stay quiet for a while,

even years, but soon enough it resurfaces and starts to cry out again. Every time it comes back, it's much louder with deeper and more intense frustration, and often at greater personal cost.

With the passing of time and the value of hindsight we come to realise that these weren't just crossroads, they were in fact turning points. Opportunities to say yes to our passion and purpose, to become the person we're meant to be and do the work that we love and are meant to do.

The seven turning points in life

The need for:

1. Purpose
2. Direction
3. Balance
4. Meaning
5. Significance
6. Re-entry
7. Crisis

These turning points often happen at certain stages in our lives, though I've regularly seen people of all ages struggle with one or more of the turning points at a stage of life you wouldn't necessarily expect. However, there are no set rules; each person is unique and needs to be listened to and understood.

Some people only experience one or two turning points throughout their whole life. Others go through each one every seven or more years. Each turning point is different and has unique needs.

Turning points can be traumatic. Twice in my life I've felt like I was trapped underground in a very tight tunnel struggling to breathe. At other times I've felt overwhelmed. Clients have reported feeling lost, confused and stuck – in fact, nearly everyone says that they feel stuck.

In the next chapter we'll look at what it takes to success-fully transition from each crossroads – you can go there now if that makes more sense for you. However, I would encourage you to take the time to read through each turning point and understand what it is that matters most to you, what it is that you need right now and which part of you needs greater expression before learning how to transition.

Let's begin…

Purpose

This turning point is the deep need to know who we are, why we're here and what it is that we're meant to do. This is a time when we wrestle with the big questions in life trying to find the answers for ourselves, going deep within us to finally figure out what we will do with our life.

It's most commonly seen in our early to mid-twenties when we're transitioning from adolescence into adulthood. It regularly appears in every decade of life. Many 50-year-olds are still trying to figure out what to do with their lives.

▶ Jayne's story: the student

I'm at university in my final year and I'll be graduating soon. My future is looming very quickly. I have big decisions to make: what to do and where to live. The one question that all of my friends are constantly asking is, 'What's next?' It seems to be the only thing we talk about. The trouble is that fewer than half of us really know what we're going to do, and I'm not one of those; I have zero idea.

I've looked online, I've talked to the careers service, but nothing seems to jump out for me. I worry that my degree is not what I want to base my whole life around. Maybe I should have studied something else. I'm not sure. I have limited work experience and the part-time jobs I've had aren't real career choices. Stacking shelves was hard, honest work, but seriously it's not what I want to do for the next 40 years.

My parents have ideas about what they think I should do with my life. They want me to go into IT or finance, or preferably IT at a bank. They believe that the only permanent jobs in the future will be in money and IT. My dad has been made redundant twice in his career and he doesn't want me to go through the same agony. Mum wishes she'd had a career and thinks that I should too. They might well be right, but what they're suggesting doesn't feel right to me. I once did a coding course, but it wasn't for me. I want to do something with greater meaning and purpose.

I feel so pressurised. There're all these voices demanding choices. I feel like all the air is going out of the room and I can't breathe. It seems totally unrealistic to know exactly what you're supposed to do with your life at 21, but there it is. I fear that if I don't get it right my whole life will be a failure; I'll get off course and end up regretting everything.

Last night I googled the five most sought-after skills for the next 10 years and the 10 hottest careers by 2020. Really, who has those skills? How are you supposed to get them? I might as well give up now.

Direction

This turning point is the deep need to know that we're on the right path for us to achieve all that we want out of life – to know where we're going, and to have the confidence to move forward in that direction.

It's the desire to become all that we can be, to achieve our deepest dreams and to do the work that we're meant to do.

This is a time when we often compare ourselves to others – when we look at the people around us as they seem to be on a straight, upward trajectory taking them towards all that they want in life and we simply can't keep up.

It's most commonly seen in our late twenties to mid-thirties when we've been working for 5–10 years and sense that our role is not the best fit for us, or that the company we work for isn't going to take us as far as we want to go and that we're not achieving all that we want out of life.

This turning point regularly appears in every decade of life.

▶ Paul's story: the graduate

I joined a solid company right out of university and was placed on their graduate placement scheme. They have hundreds of applicants every year from all over the world for only 50 places, and I was one of the lucky ones.

The first year was incredible. I worked in two different

departments – marketing and logistics – and seemed to do well in both. The logistics manager said I had a real talent for managing data and projects and had a bright future ahead of me. Throughout the year we were constantly told that we were the future of the company, that we could achieve anything and go as far as we wanted. I was stoked. This was definitely the right company for me.

I expected to be placed permanently in the logistics department but was pleasantly surprised to be placed in consultancy. I guess because of my research abilities. It was the most sought-after department to work in.

At first it was great; I got to work on some high-profile projects and did everything that was asked of me. However, after two years I began to feel that something wasn't right. It was a growing sense that this wasn't the right path for me. Consultancy came with a high salary and I didn't complain, but the hours were ridiculously long and I often had to work weekends, but I always felt it was leading somewhere and one day things would get better.

I feel as if I have plateaued. I am no longer invited to client meetings. I am involved with research only. I enjoy researching but I never get to do anything with the data: I don't get to make recommendations or work on imple-mentations, and I haven't had any promotions for the last two years.

People who joined at the same time as me are doing much better – they've had promotions and they get to do much more interesting work. I feel stuck and that I'm going nowhere. Friends say I shouldn't complain as I am making great money, work for a prestigious company and have a bright future, but I'm not so sure. I don't know whether to stay or go. If I stay something needs to change, but I don't know what, and if I go what on earth could I do? I feel very stuck and overwhelmed.

Balance

This turning point is the need to find and achieve balance in our lives when we're wrestling with the competing demands of social, family, career and personal needs; simultaneously trying to juggle multiple activities.

This is a time when we can feel overwhelmed, out of control and run down. We often see this portrayed in films as the American 'soccer mom' taking the kids to school, running the home, doing the shopping, cooking meals, trying to be active in church, taking her daughter to practice after school, attending games on Saturday and trying to keep her son off the computer...

She helps with homework, volunteers with the PTA,

bakes cakes for the church fundraiser and is regularly called upon to listen to her friends' problems. She's trying to stay fit and healthy by going to the gym, but that's an ever-losing battle. She wants to stay attractive to her husband but increasingly she feels he's not that interested anymore. She prays to God and drinks gin.

This is most commonly seen in our mid-thirties to early forties. It can appear in any decade of life but is mainly associated with the mid-years.

▶ Cathy's story: the worn-out mum

We'd been trying to get pregnant for over two years and, when it happened, I was overjoyed. When Tara was born, I left work and concentrated on being her carer and running our home. It was a joint decision – I didn't feel pressurised to do it and in fact it was something that I had always wanted.

Initially there were some teething problems. I wasn't used to having to depend on someone else for money. Asking for it when I needed something was difficult and very stressful. It still is. James, my husband, would come home after work and expect me to cook and take care of him. He would forget that I had also put in a 10-hour day.

After trying so hard for Tara it was a complete surprise to then get pregnant a year later with twins. I was overjoyed and scared at the same time wondering how on earth I would cope. When the girls were born it was wonderful. Their different personalities had us feeling like the luckiest people on earth.

The first year was hard work looking after three children, much harder than I thought it would be, but it was when Tara started school that my life began to really unwind.

I would have to get her ready for school and compete with the rush hour traffic to get her there on time. Then come back home and clear up before taking the twins to nursery. Then I'd go on this mad whirlwind of shopping, unpacking, stacking the dishwasher, cleaning the house, washing the clothes, picking up the twins, feeding them, entertaining them, collecting Tara, making snacks, cooking dinner, tidying the house, bathing the kids, getting their clothes ready for the next day and then putting them all to bed.

After that I'd be buying presents online for the endless birthday parties the kids were invited to, supporting James with his career issues and helping him pack as he got ready to go on another business trip. He doesn't want sex very often these days and I worry about that. I feel unattractive, unwanted and overwhelmed. I feel that I am losing sight of myself. Will this ever change?

Meaning

This turning point is the deep need to know that what we do matters; that our work and effort has a meaning and purpose and is of value.

It's most commonly seen in midlife; typically our mid-forties when we've been working for 20 or more years and haven't been unhappy but have a growing sensation that there must be more to life and that what we do doesn't really matter. It's often accompanied with a level of distress that it's too late to do something else, with a concern that, if we don't, the next 20 years won't be any different.

▶David's story: midlife crisis

I'm a middle manager for a tech company. I'm increasingly bored at work and feel that I'm just going through the motions. I'm not underperforming enough that I'm likely to lose my job, but I'm also not performing well enough for my company to want to promote or invest in me. I often travel and spend nights away from home. I'm increasingly feeling anger and resentment towards others who are doing well. Something needs to change, but I'm dammed if I know what.

To be honest, I haven't really been very happy throughout my working life and I have always felt that I could have achieved a lot more and often compare myself to others.

My home life is static. My teenagers don't want to spend time with me, and I don't feel like I'm particularly welcome. I often daydream and long for a great adventure. I want to be respected and to know that I'm doing something that's important, and that people appreciate me for who I am.

Significance

This turning point is the deep need to know that what we've achieved has made an impact and that our lives matter. Often, we've been successful but question whether what we've achieved is of any significant value.

This is a time when our success fails to satisfy us at a deeper level and can even feel superficial. It most commonly presents itself in our fifties. It can also appear at times after we've achieved an unusual level of success.

▶ Meera's story: success without satisfaction

I am not your typical Asian woman. I'm stereotypically driven and ambitious, but I've always known that I wanted to be more than a wife and mother.

I saw my father work long hours in the family shop and not have much to show for it as well as struggle with his health. My mother took care of the family but was always unhappy, wanting more from life but never pursuing her dreams. I was determined not to follow in their footsteps and instead carve out my own career path.

I've always had an innate ability with marketing, especially creative storytelling. After university I worked for the marketing department of a large national company for five years before leaving to start my own marketing agency. Over the next 25 years I grew the company to incredible levels of success, had a family and achieved many of my life goals.

In my fifties I began to feel that life was passing me by. I had practically everything that anyone could want, but when I woke up, I had this feeling in the pit of my stomach that something was wrong.

As I reflect on my life, I question the value of the work I've done. I've helped companies make millions through creative marketing and advertising, but I can't help feeling that the world didn't need more of what we help sell. I worry that I have failed to achieve anything of great significance. It bothers me a lot. I want my family to be proud of what I've done and I hope it's not too late.

Re-entry

This turning point is the deep need to find a new sense

of purpose and direction. It's the desire to know that we still have value and, despite our age, can still positively contribute to the world around us.

This occurs around the time when we're about to retire and transition into a new stage of life, or generally within two to three years post-retirement. It most commonly presents itself in our sixties and predominantly impacts men.

▶ Robert's story: recently retired

I'd been in the civil service for over 30 years. My pension's good and I have considerable savings and investments. With no mortgage my wife and I were very much looking forward to retirement – to putting our feet up and enjoying the finer things in life.

I retired two years ago and I remember being sent on a retirement seminar where we heard from financial advisors, doctors and even travel agents on how to best enjoy our retirement. There was one speaker who told us that we needed to have a purpose in life – a reason to get up each day and get out of the house. He shared stories of people who really struggled.

Initially retirement was fantastic – much better than I thought. The first six months were amazing. I slept in some days and got up early on others. It was great not to have any routine or structure. We had days out, ate out and visited family and friends. My wife took up some classes at the local college and encouraged me to join their 'wine appreciation for beginners' course.

I began to struggle after 10 months. I started having difficulty getting out of bed and began to lose interest in the things I normally found stimulating. I lost my appetite and stopped shaving, which sounds silly but I'd shaved every day of my life.

I missed the routine and structure of my work, particularly the planning and resourcing of big projects. That always gave me a sense of meaning; that what I was doing was important and something that we had to get right because people's lives and well-being depended on it.

I increasingly feel despondent. I enjoy the grandchildren's visits, but I don't want to spend the next 20 years just visiting garden centres and market towns. My wife's very happy with it all, but it's not enough for me. I want to feel connected to a bigger purpose. I know I still have much more to give and, despite my age, feel that I can make a significant contribution.

Crisis

This turning point is when we struggle to come to terms with a sudden change in our circumstances combined with a perceived inability to change them.

We've been going through life with its usual joys and challenges and have dealt with previous turning points. Then, and without warning, we experience a major crisis in our life:

- redundancy
- health issues
- relational breakdown
- financial pressures
- death of a loved one
- anxiety, sadness or depression

When we hit a crisis it feels like a body blow, where the air is knocked out of us and we can't breathe. We get stuck, feel overwhelmed and have no idea what to do next.

For many people these crises are short-lived. They come and go and hopefully life returns to normal. This is the desire to get back on to the wheel of life and to play the game again.

Crisis can happen at any time and without any advance

warning. This makes it particularly painful as we struggle to understand why it's happening.

►Angela's story: career crisis

A year ago, I had to leave the company I'd been with for five years, the last two of which had become quite unbearable as I felt bullied by my boss and humiliated by my male colleagues.

I worked in the IT department of a large organisation working in cybersecurity. It is a predominantly male environment but, increasingly, we're seeing more women enter this field. Everything had been going well until I started noticing that we weren't adequately protecting our networks. I told my boss and he seemed quite supportive and encouraged me to make the necessary changes.

In making the changes I found that the gaps in security were due to errors by my colleagues. I informed my boss who wasn't happy that I was accusing my colleagues of incompetence. I wasn't trying to make trouble, I just wanted to do my job and protect our systems.

He must have spoken to my colleagues because, soon after, the bullying began. At first it was passive-aggressive; snide remarks and not being invited to meetings or copied into emails. Once I was publicly criticised in a meeting by my boss and everybody laughed. That gave everyone a free license to abuse me as often as they wanted.

I went to HR but was told I was being too sensitive. Shortly after I was marked down in my appraisal and given an official warning. It was a struggle to work there. Each day was more difficult, and my health began to suffer – I wasn't able to sleep properly for a year.

After months of complaining to HR, I was offered a deal to go but had to sign a contract saying that I couldn't talk about the company, the allegations or the settlement. I feel as if they've gotten away with bullying and I've been gagged.

Initially it felt wonderful to have left, but I haven't been able to find another job. I don't know if my name's been blacklisted, because, with my qualifications, it should be relatively easy to find another role. Now I'm under great financial pressure and I worry about not being able to pay my mortgage. I constantly doubt myself and have low self-esteem. I'm exploring a career change but it's not working, and I feel useless and don't know what to do. I'm stuck.

Your Story: Where Are You?

Often when I give my talk on Crossroads and Turning Points, people come up to me afterwards and say how much one or more of the stories deeply resonated with them. I remember John saying that it was as if I'd told the entire story of his life and he was keen to know how to move forward and finally live the life that he most wanted.

That's the amazing thing: no matter where you are right now, no matter how difficult your situation may seem, change is possible. You have within you all you need to see your life turnaround and finally begin to live the life you have always wanted, do the work that you love and are meant to do, and be the person you were born to be – fearless, brave and confident.

In Part 2 of this book I'll introduce you to seven steps that will lead you quickly and powerfully from a place of feeling stuck and confused to a place of clarity about where you're going in life and what you need to do to get there, giving you the confidence to take the necessary action required.

Over time I have come to realise that the doubt and confusion we experience at a crossroads are in fact messages from our inner self wanting us to know that something is not right and that we have yet to take hold of the life we're meant to live and that is available to us. In the next chapter we'll explore what we need to do in order to get moving again.

CHAPTER 3

Disconnected

Being stuck at a crossroads is a sure sign that we're not living the life we want and that is available to us or doing the work we're meant to do. It's a message that it's time to change.

The primary reason we're stuck, overwhelmed and confused is that there is a disconnect between our heart – what we really want, love to do and what matters most – and our mind – what we believe is possible, what we deserve and is permissible.

Our heart needs to follow its passions, pursue its calling and focus on what matters most and, in order to do so, it requires the mind to be in alignment providing supportive beliefs that tell us that what we desire is possible, that we deserve it and fully expect that it will happen. If we are to make our dreams happen, we definitely need to know that we are intrinsically worthy of those dreams, wants and desires.

The second reason is that there is a misalignment with what we really want out of life and work and the path we're travelling on to get there.

We want to create, to birth our ideas and concepts and share them with others through the work that we do. We are each motivated with different vocational preferences, gifts and abilities. We also have dreams and callings of how we can best use our gifts in the service of others; sometimes referred to as our 'mission' in life, the people we serve, the problems we solve and the outcomes we want to create.

We have goals that we want to fulfil and each of us is on a path and trajectory which we hope will allow us to do the work we're meant to do, live outrageously, be the best version of ourselves and achieve our dreams and goals.

The challenge is when what we're doing and the path we're following don't take us in the direction that we want to go.

When the heart and mind are connected and working as one, and when our gifts, talents and work are in alignment, we move effortlessly towards our dreams and desires. However, when there's disconnect and misalignment we falter, and progress becomes slow and difficult. When this happens, we struggle and everything feels like an uphill battle. We end up settling for less, but the heart never forgets what it wants and will keep speaking to us, reminding us of who we are and why we're here. That voice, once loud and clear, may become quiet, but it never goes away.

When we hear that voice, we will look at life and see the ever-widening gap between what we really want and what we have and, if we're not vigilant, a malaise enters the heart. There is nothing like the slow, sad heartache you experience when what you hope for is seemingly always out of reach. However, recognising that there is a gap between where we are and what we want provides us with the starting point to get there. The power of this book and the principles and steps it provides, is that no matter where you're at, if you follow and implement the steps you will begin to create the necessary change to move you forwards in the direction of your dreams.

Our Influences

Throughout our early life our beliefs were shaped and influenced by our experiences and those closest to us. We were directly told by others what to believe, think and how to behave. At school we were told to sit down, be quiet and do what we were told. Religion offered us more of the same. At home we were taught to do what we were told but we were more likely to copy the behaviours of our parents, both good and bad.

People constantly model their world view of what's

acceptable and permissible through their actions and decisions. My father came from India, where there was no social security system. The belief was that you have to take care of yourself, because nobody else will. Therefore education becomes really important because it gives you the best opportunity to get a good, safe and secure job that will provide for you and your loved ones throughout your life. That belief comes at a price, because for many it requires that you suppress your passions and callings in order to do what pays the best. Growing up I felt incredible pressure from my parents to do well academically, especially in Science, but I wasn't good at Science and so never did very well. The pressure to perform made me feel like a failure. My English mother said she felt the same kind of pressure from her parents, which led to her experiencing many years of unhappiness. It's a cycle.

What we accept and believe as children will generally stay with us throughout our lives, shaping our thinking, choices and behaviour. Carl Jung said that, 'Nothing affects a child quite like the unlived life of a parent.' It's not only our parents, but also our educational institutions and society with its norms and expectations, that shape our early thinking.

Family of origin

Our parents often live out their unlived lives through us, their children, projecting on to us their hopes and dreams, as well as their fears prejudices and values. We have little choice but to blindly follow their lead and do what they do, make the same decisions and eventually become them. How many of us have looked in the mirror or heard our own voice and thought, 'Oh my goodness, I look and sound like my parents'?

As children we don't know what's useful and what's unhelpful – we accept it all and it becomes part of our human operating system until it no longer serves us and, one day, our true self rises up and says 'no more' and demands to be heard and understood.

Kriti, a 30-something Indian woman, came to coaching feeling confused, mentally exhausted and deeply frustrated with her life. She was an IT professional developing her own successful business, but something was missing. There was a lack of peace and joy in her life.

As we talked, she shared about being raised as a girl in India. From an early age, she had been raised with a single goal – to be a good wife and mother;

like her mother and her mother's mother, and all of the mothers before them. Yet she'd seen how unhappy her mother was, how distant her father had been and how unhappy they had been as a married couple.

Kriti saw how her mother had to depend on her father for everything and how unhappy that made her as a result.

Our core values are developed in both positive and negative processing environments. In negative processing environments we are exposed to something negative (not necessarily destructive) and, as a result, we question what we see and begin to value the opposite. In Kriti's case, independence.

Her mother-in-law constantly criticised her saying that she should stay at home and take care of her husband and children. She accused her of being a bad mother and bringing shame to the family, which brought Kriti to breaking point.

She was at the turning point called 'Balance' (see page 32), trying to juggle the demands of life: both her and her husband's career, the needs of her family and her own personal needs. The balls had been successfully spinning in the air for a while, years in fact, but now they had all come crashing down.

Kriti began to understand that there was a disconnect between what she wanted and what she believed was expected of her. As she began to let go of the limiting beliefs that she'd accepted as true and began to intentionally build her life around her passions, values and calling, the stress and confusion melted away.

What Kriti experienced is also available for you. This book will guide you to a place of personal freedom, free from the false expectations of others. Keep going – you'll get there.

Education

Most of us receive some thirteen years of education from the ages of five to eighteen. Some then go on to receive a further three years' university undergraduate education and some receive another two to four years of postgraduate study. That's nearly a quarter of our lives spent in education!

Many countries have significant variations in how they educate their children, from the ages at which they start and the subjects they teach to how they teach their children based on their unique learning styles. All create their curriculum based on the needs of government and business.

Business informs government which skills and knowledge they need young people to have when they leave education. Marketplace survival depends on having an adequately skilled workforce. Governments need the taxes that businesses provide. A healthy economy requires growing businesses and job creation.

Government creates a national curriculum that schools need to teach young people and audit it relentlessly. Young people are then asked to make choices based on what is often a limited curriculum. For some children this works. For many it fails them.

Many never know or are never encouraged to discover their innate talents or to dive deeply into the subjects that interest and fascinate them. Society values intellectual ability over all other abilities and children are measured by regular examinations. Those who do well are placed in advanced learning groups. Those who don't often feel they've failed.

Sandeep said that he never forgot the shame he felt in Year 8 when all of the pupils were told which streams they would be place in for the following year and he was placed in the lowest. He remembers the other students laughing as each name was read out for the very last class.

Vocational abilities are often considered of lesser value. Those who are naturally gifted with their hands are often inadequately served. How many children blessed with incredible vocational gifts and talents get left behind?

When it comes to choosing a career path, most never receive enough exposure to a wide range of jobs and industries. Few get meaningful work experience or placements. Very few are given sufficient space and encouragement to explore what it is that they are good at and enjoy doing. Over the years I have had the privilege of meeting a growing number of school careers advisers who are brilliant, love what they do and excel at helping young people. They rarely have the resources that are needed.

Rob came to coaching because he was graduating from university in the next two months. He should have been excited, but was feeling terrified because he was not sure what to do next. He was finishing his degree in Business Studies but discovered in his first year that he didn't really like business. He wanted to quit and do something else, but his father repeatedly told him that it would give him the best opportunities after graduation.

Rob wanted to study Sociology to follow his

fascination about how communities grow and develop. He once read an Internet article about a coal mine that was closed and the detrimental social and economic effects it had on the entire community and how they bounced back. He'd like to know why. At school they didn't teach Sociology. He's not sure his father would have encouraged it even if they did.

Rob quickly came to realise that even though he didn't have the chance to study what he really wanted, or if his father didn't approve, he now gets to decide for himself what he really wants to do. He went and chatted to those miners and was amazed at their resilience and now he's training in Applied Psychology to be a creativity facilitator.

Social norms

When my parents' generation started working, they fully expected to work all their lives for one or possibly two companies. They believed that the company would take care of them, and that if they worked hard, they would progress. They believed that they should get married, buy a house, have kids and take care of them. They believed that retirement was when you really got to have fun and enjoy life. They lived for the future.

When my generation started work, we had the same expectations as my parents' generation – because that's what we were told – but the world began to change and, with it, the world of work and how we lived changed forever, and not always for the better. The Internet and technology created a global market, which meant that entire industries disappeared, and business models ceased to work or completely changed. Work could be performed anywhere in the world. Your job could be and was often replaced by someone on the other side of the world.

We worked from home and boundary lines got blurred. We often worked a long distance away from where we lived. We became part of two communities – our geographical neighbourhood and those we worked with. Often, we increasingly felt most apart from those we lived closest to.

We were prepared for a world that no longer existed. We tried marriage but increasingly failed. We raised kids in two homes and lived for the weekend.

My children's generation – Generation Z – has completely different expectations about work and life. Like Millennials they fully expect to have multiple jobs and careers. Many are indifferent towards marriage; after all it didn't work out very well for many of their parents. They don't expect to own property. Their communities are often found online. They have hundreds of 'friends' but diminishing numbers of real conversations.

They see themselves as self-employed even when working for a company. They want to work with meaning and purpose; they want to truly develop their skills and follow their passions. They want to start businesses. They see the world as a village. They are passionate about solving the problems that their parents and grandparents created. They want to follow their passion, live on purpose and do work that matters to them. They live for now.

Amanda is 18 and wants to go to university – she's not here in the room with us, but her mother is sat in front of me asking if I would coach her.

'I'll pay you whatever you want, please help us.'

'What's the challenge and how can I help?' I ask.

'She wants to study Drama and be an actress. I need you to coach her to become a lawyer,' her mother replies.

'Why do you want her to become a lawyer?' I ask.

'Because we didn't spend all that money at private school for her to waste her life on acting. What on earth would they think at the Bridge Club?'

Amanda – I tried to talk to your mother, but I'm

pretty sure that I failed to get through. I hope that you got to follow your dreams.

Social expectations vary from community to community and from decade to decade. What doesn't change, however, is the pressure we feel to conform.

My friends told me about how their daughter was being bullied at school. Knowing that she was a very sociable and well-liked child I was shocked. Apparently, the reason was that she was the only child in her class who hadn't been to Disney World.

Growing up as a mixed-race child, I experienced such vile racism on a daily basis that I begged my parents to let me change my Indian name from Sunil to Neil. The pressure and desire to conform and be accepted by others was immense. The TV programme *Goodness Gracious Me* got it right.

There are countless other influences that shape our beliefs, in particular religion, the media and the arts and entertainment industry – all working to create positive and negative world views.

All of these influences affect how we think about ourselves, the world and our place in it. They shape what we believe is possible and, to one degree or another, help or hinder our progress in life. When we're at a crossroads, we're being given a message by our inner self that something isn't right, that we're disconnected and misaligned.

At these moments we have the opportunity to stop and pause and take the time to look deep within ourselves and ask what it is that we love and want to do with our precious few moments here on earth. We can then develop the belief systems that support that and let go of those that hold us back, don't serve us well and limit what we're capable of achieving, especially all of the false evidence that appears real, as well as the false expectations of others that have the power to stop us becoming all that we can be and enjoying the life we deserve to live.

Later we'll look at how to let go of the lies we've believed about ourselves and how we can reconnect our heart with our head to get clear about what we want in life and develop the confidence to take the inspired action to make it happen.

In the meantime, the next chapter explores how we can align what we want with what we do and how we live. This is your time and it's time to fly.

CHAPTER 4

Alignment

A few years ago, I decided to give my garden a complete makeover and enlisted the help of a good friend. Together we first designed and then created my dream garden. We dug new planting areas and borders, built a shed and created a pathway. I bought loads of plants and shrubs and, over the course of six days, we planted, fed and watered them. The garden looked great.

However, in less than two weeks, a number of the plants began to whither and some died. Not knowing what to do, I called on the wisdom of a professional horticulturist friend of mine. His diagnosis was that many of the plants and shrubs weren't planted according to the conditions in which they best grow and flourish. So we moved some from direct sunlight to shade; others from shade to areas of bright sunlight; and others to windier areas of the garden. We had to give away some plants as they wouldn't do well in the naturally clay-based soil. After improving the soil and replanting, I'm happy to report that the plants grew and flourished and gave us many years of joy.

Just as plants need to be correctly aligned with the right soil and natural environmental dynamics to success-fully grow and flourish, so do humans need to be aligned with 12 core dynamics if we want to live a life of meaning, purpose and contribution, of adventure and personal growth, connection and success. When we are aligned with these, we build a solid foundation from which can truly enjoy a life full of happiness and free from worry and anxiety.

The 12 Core Dynamics

Many of the 12 core dynamics outlined below will be familiar to you and some no doubt will be new. They're easy to grasp and reasonably self-explanatory, and are the secret to life and career happiness. Once you understand these dynamics and how they shape your thinking and action, you'll be equipped to make positive changes that will increase your happiness and effectiveness. You'll get unstuck, live from a place of purpose and have the confidence to move in the direction of your dreams. We'll go into much further detail about some of these dynamics in the coming chapters.

More in-depth information and exercises can be found in a free workbook, which can be downloaded from: www.routesuk.com

ABUNDANT LIFE MODEL

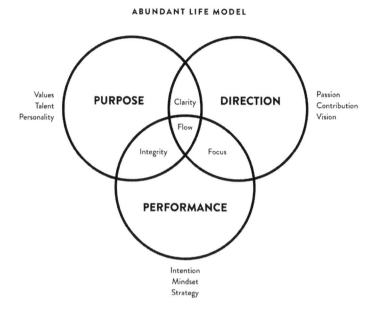

Values

This first dynamic is about aligning ourselves with what matters most – our values.

Our values are our deepest-held individual beliefs about what matters most and give our lives meaning. They are generally shaped in our formative childhood years and become the guide to how we think and make decisions. We have three levels of values: universal, adopted and core values.

Universal values are those values that all of us accept as moral, ethical and important – life is better when we live this way. These typically include values such as love, happiness, family, peace and prosperity. Most people around the world believe these to be of great importance and want them for themselves. There are times in history when governments and regimes take these away from people, failing to recognise that people still want to live that way and will die to protect what matters most. These values may also be so important to us as to be part of our core values.

Our adopted values are those we choose for ourselves based on the cultural and societal values that we grew up with and continue to experience on a daily basis in the communities in which we live and work. Every decade, postcode and generation decides that some things are more important than others. There were times in history when we thought racism, prejudice and inequality were acceptable and, thankfully, now we don't. Adopted values may not really be at the core of who we are and what we really consider as important. This is often seen in the individual who highly values monetary success but later in midlife realises that their money hasn't bought them happiness and discards that value in favour of something more meaningful. Adopted values change.

Core values lie at the heart of all that we think, say and do, and shape our every decision – all that we think and do. They lie at the heart of who we are and reflect our innermost being and shape our behaviour. Typically, most people have only three to five core values. That doesn't mean to say that nothing else is important, but these few values are the *most* important. Values often change in their importance to us throughout our life but core values rarely, if ever, change.

Talent

The second dynamic is about aligning with our motivational abilities – our gifts and talents.

Our talents are those abilities that we both enjoy using and are good at. They are different from skills, which are abilities in which we have a high, or at least repeatable, level of competence but may not necessarily love and enjoy doing – think of ironing, a skill most of us have, but seldom enjoy doing for long.

Then there are gifts and strengths. Our gifts occur when clusters of unique talents combine together to create something even more dynamic with a driving motivation to use them. Everyone will have a favourite musician who they think has a gift for music. That gift for music is actually a cluster of three talents working together: pitch (the ability to hear the difference between notes); rhythm (the ability to keep time and move in flow with the beat); and auditory memory (the ability to memorise complex melodies).

The musician needs an outlet for their talent – composing, playing or singing – and learns how to do something that with practice then becomes a skill. Over many years of practice that musician turns that skill into a strength.

Aligning with our motivational abilities and finding an outlet for what we are deeply and truly motivated to do offers us the greatest opportunity for career satisfaction.

Personality

The third dynamic is about aligning with how we naturally think, feel and interact with the world around us – our personality. It's about aligning with our preferred environments in which we naturally grow and flourish. We do this through discovering and then aligning with our unique personal style where we can perform at our best.

Our gifts and talents are what we do, and our personality is how we do it. Our personal style is part of our uniqueness – it defines how we think, feel and interact with the world around us. It's how we best function and get things done. Our personal style is a set of preferences, including well-known preferences for:

- introversion and extroversion
- working in a structured or unstructured manner
- working with people, information, ideas or objects
- being a generalist or a specialist
- operating with a preference for a long- or short-term focus

It also includes preferences for our living and working environments, including space, light and much more.

Aligning with our personal preferences puts us in a position where we can experience a greater sense of flow. Staying outside of this area diminishes flow, creates tension and stress, and often can lead to dis-ease.

Purpose

The fourth dynamic is about aligning with the driving rationale behind how and why we want to use our gifts and talents – our purpose. It's what author and motivational speaker, Simon Sinek, calls our 'why'. It's the place where our values and talents merge into a single driving force that shapes and influences all of our efforts.

I have helped hundreds of individuals and companies to discover their purpose – their 'why'. Each purpose has been incredibly different and uniquely personal. We'll explore this fully in Chapter 9 and I will take you through an exercise to help you discover and live your why.

Passion

The fifth dynamic is about aligning with those interests that energise us – our passion.

Passion is the desire to give our time, talent and energy to what matters most. At the same time, it energises us. It's rare to have a single passion and, in all the years working with people to help them find and follow their passions, I've never met one person with only one single driving passion. Nearly everyone I've worked with has had a broad range of subjects and activities that they loved to engage with. They often struggle to decide which they should focus on.

We'll explore this more in Chapter 6 where we'll learn how to align with our passions in order to re-energise and enter flow.

Contribution

The sixth dynamic is about aligning our purpose with our mission, by which I mean the people we are inspired to serve, the problems we are motivated to solve and the outcomes we create – our contribution.

Contribution is the desire to want to make a difference; to use our gifts and talents to help others and to know that our efforts have been of value to others and, increasingly, to the world around us.

Whether that's a desire to raise kind and caring children, to find a cure for cancer, to build beautiful homes and buildings, to write a bestseller or care for the dying, each of us has an intrinsic motivation to want to help. Some of us have a desire to contribute on a global scale, while others wish to help a single person. Our unique contribution doesn't have to be big, spiritual or clever. When we're fully aligned with the contribution we want to make, we experience 'flow'.

We'll explore this much more in Chapter 11 where we'll seek to define the situations and audiences in which we find the greatest fulfilment.

Vision

The seventh dynamic is about aligning our goals for all aspects of our life – what we want to do, be and have – into a single integrated and compelling picture of our desired future – our vision.

Vision is the desire to work towards a future reality that we want to create for ourselves and those we love.

People often fail to fully bring their life and work into alignment because they have a vision that is largely focused on a single area of their lives – mainly their career – and does not blend together all the key areas of their life, such as health, finances, career, family and friends, personal development, significant other, fun and recreation, and contribution to society.

Having a personal vision gives us our own internal GPS system that continually guides us towards the destination we want to get to. It creates a North Star that keeps us from wandering aimlessly, keeps us on track and prompts us when we get lost, gently bringing us back on course towards our dreams and desires. Our vision is our guiding light helping us to understand where we are and what we have to do to get back to where we want to go.

The biggest regret of the dying is not what they did do but what they didn't do, the risks they didn't take. A personal whole-of-life vision is the first step to ensuring this doesn't happen.

Direction

The eighth dynamic is about aligning with our strategic path – our direction. Our direction in life – the path that we're travelling on – will allow us, or at least give us the potential, to engage with our purpose, fulfil our mission, enjoy our passions and take us towards our goals (vision).

Being on the right path offers you the opportunity to look forward to going to work and enjoy what you do; to keep growing by regularly learning new skills and gaining in knowledge; to enjoy the people you work with; to know that what you do is important and that/how it contributes to the bigger picture, and every day you feel you're getting closer to your goals.

When you're not on the right path you wake up each day with a sense of dread. You don't enjoy what you do and feel stagnant. You're not learning anything new and, if you are, you're not enjoying what you're learning. You may no longer enjoy being with your colleagues and you don't feel that what you're doing is important or contributes to anything bigger. You don't feel you are getting any closer to your goals – if you have any.

Intention

The ninth dynamic is about aligning a clear mental picture of what we're wanting with a full expectation that it will happen – our intention. Our intention is the gateway to manifesting our dreams and desires.

Setting an intention is also about resolve, but it's not

about setting goals and working tirelessly to make them happen. Goal-setting is useful and important, but intention is much more than that; it's about aligning with the creative laws and principles that govern our universe.

Napoleon Hill famously said, 'What the mind can conceive and believe, the mind can achieve.'

Intention is the starting point for everything that happens; every dream and goal. It's also known as the 'Law of Attraction' – you attract everything that you think about with feeling – and sometimes it's referred to as the 'Law of First Creation' – the law that states that everything is created twice: first in the mind and then in the physical. The chair you're sitting on now was once in the mind of the designer. She had a clear picture in her mind of what she wanted to create. The same is true of the building you're in or looking at. The architect didn't just start throwing bricks in every direction hoping that the building would happen. No, he sat down with the client, listened to their needs, wants and constraints, and, from that, created the design in his mind, then on to paper, then into engineering plans and then, and only then, was the building actually built.

As Walt Disney said, 'If you can dream it you can do it.'

Mindset

The tenth dynamic is about aligning our beliefs about who we are and what's possible and permissible, with the desires of our heart, in order to create and release positive intentions – our mindset.

A positive mindset is essential to create the necessary beliefs so that we can reconnect with and support the intentions of our hearts.

Developing the right mindset and worldview allows us to do what others say isn't possible. It allows us to shake off the limiting beliefs that hold us back and stretch our comfort zone around what we can achieve. It allows us to throw off the expectations of others about what they say we can and can't do.

Having the right mindset ensures that we will no longer be double-minded in everything that we do. We'll stop doubting our intentions and our ability to make them happen. When we have a clear picture of the life we want and the work that we love and are meant to do, combined with a strong and positive mindset that says not only we can do it but fully expects it to happen, we will move from a place of continual indecision to a place where we are able to make quick decisions and take daily inspired action towards our goals.

71

Strategy

The eleventh dynamic is about aligning our actions with our intentions; it's about how we make things happen – our strategy. Our strategy ensures that we focus on what's both urgent and important, what matters most and what needs to be done at any given time. It's also learning to trust our intuition about what we should do next.

Strategy is the desire to make things happen. It is not just about breaking our goals down into steps and then putting them in our diary and on to our to-do list. It's about taking inspired and intuitive action – listening to your intuition and engaging with what you feel led to do and receiving guidance through the serendipities that happen as a result.

Over the years, I have worked with hundreds of leaders, many on the edge of burnout, all with huge and ever-growing to-do lists, and yet never seemingly making sufficient progress towards their vision. When they learn to slow down, breathe and get out of their heads, and create the necessary space to listen to their intuition and learn to trust in what they receive and act on it, amazing things happen; they experience serendipity and are able to achieve far more than they ever thought possible, in less time and with fewer resources.

The type of strategy is about is taking inspired and intuitive action.

Performance

The twelfth, and final, dynamic is about aligning our purpose and direction with our intentions, mindset and actions – our performance. This is about ensuring that every step we take is moving us in the direction we want to go.

Performance is the desire to achieve our goals. It's the sum total of all that we're putting out into the world. Not a 'success or fail' kind of bullish performance, or the drive to be number one, although that's okay if that's what you want; it's the joy and peace we feel in our core, knowing that what we want is seeking us and is gently and rapidly unfolding before us. The joy that comes when you succeed with your first attempt at something.

Performance is also about accepting that things don't work out as you thought they would, and that failure is a necessary step towards success. This dynamic is also about learning from the experience when things don't go according to plan. It's knowing that when people let you down, when you let yourself down and when you make mistakes, there is always something to learn. Failure only happens when you fail to learn and adapt.

When we stop striving for perfect performance and learn to trust and be guided by our intuition, we will find that there is a peace that comes from knowing that when we are actively partnering with our intuition and the principles of the universe, everything negative and unexpected that happens will always turn around for our benefit. This is important. Knowing our purpose and direction is good, but it's turning our vision into reality that is the real key. Moving from a fear-based level of performance to one of guided intuition free from fear is when we'll see more than we ever thought possible become true. Part 2 will take you through seven steps to show you how to do this.

Getting into Alignment and Experiencing Flow

The good news is that no matter what you're going through right now, you can begin the process to realign and experience the joy that comes through stepping into flow. It's not going to cost you anything except time and energy, and the great news is that I'm going to show you how to get much more of both.

It can take up to seven weeks to get into alignment the first time you do it, although you'll start to experience incredible benefits straightaway. Once you've experienced what it really feels like to be in flow, you'll want to stay there forever.

If, like many of us, the busyness of life and the cares of the world take you out of flow, having learnt the process to get into alignment and flow, you can get back there almost immediately. You are only ever one intention away.

Taking time out each year to deliberately align and experience greater levels of flow will take you to places you never thought of or imagined. I call these purpose projects (#PurposeProjects) and we'll look more at them in Chapter 12.

The second part of this book offers you seven steps to take you on a journey of aligning with the 12 dynamics and getting into flow. Let's begin by slowing down.

PART 2

Seven Steps to Purpose

CHAPTER 5

Step 1: Slow Down

In order for us to reconnect and come back into alignment, and therefore for change to happen, we first need to create sufficient space to allow this to happen effortlessly. That requires us to have enough opportunities to think, create and embrace new possibilities. Which means finding more time. We all have 24 hours in a day. No one has fewer, or more. How we fill each of those precious hours is what's important.

Most of us don't wake up to an alarm clock anymore, but instead to an app on our mobile phone. We reach out, turn it off and then, without thinking, begin the unconscious routine of clicking from one app to another – checking our emails, social media feeds, our calendar, the weather and the news – all before getting out of bed. If we don't do it before we get out of bed, we do it soon enough over breakfast and coffee – or we do all three while travelling to work.

Technology was created to make life easier for us and to give us more time, which we then sadly use to do ever more.

We're running on autopilot. We are permanently

connected to the Web. We're busy and we're overloaded. Freelancers complain that they can never switch off; they're always working. Many office workers are saying the same thing, receiving requests from their colleagues and bosses at night and over the weekend. 24/7/365 – we never switch off.

In the UK we work the longest hours in Europe and, when we leave the office at what should be the end of the day, we're simply never done. We check our emails on the way home, and again when we get there, and several times throughout the evening. We work on projects when we should be relaxing and spending our time and energy with the people who matter. We're always thinking about what to do next and so we seldom switch off.

We're constantly bombarded with information – emails, adverts, likes and requests –which requires us to make endless choices, all of which drains our limited energy and means we are constantly tired. Our modern pace of life is simply not sustainable. We're getting less sleep and we're experiencing incredibly high levels of stress. We're nearly always running to catch up.

The modern dilemma of FOMO (fear of missing out) is a constant devil on our shoulder, driving us relentlessly, telling us we need more and more. Consequently, we seldom take the time to stop and consider what we want out of life and what's most important, or ponder the really big questions such as, 'How much is enough?' Yet we all have physical, mental and emotional limitations and, when we reach them and go past them, repeatedly going overdrawn on our time and energy, something breaks and forces us to stop and reconsider where we're going in life. But often it's too late, and change then comes at a huge price.

We need to create adequate space between our workload and our capacity to handle it. We need a buffer zone – space to be able to think and process what we're learning and experiencing. We need time to handle the urgent and the unexpected. We need breathing space, more physical, spiritual, emotional and financial space, and more time.

When we deliberately carve out more time and space, we experience a multitude of benefits:

- We are happier.
- We're healthier.
- We experience greater joy and peace.
- We have less stress.
- We have time to enjoy our relationships.
- We're able to contribute more (the paradox of doing less enables us to do more).

- We are more able to move from trying to survive to being able to thrive.

Let's look at what we need to do to create space in our lives.

Slow Down

We live life at such a ferocious pace. We're constantly multitasking. Designer Paolo Cardini says, 'People aren't just cooking anymore – they're cooking, texting, talking on the phone, watching YouTube and uploading photos of the awesome meal they've made to social media.'

We're constantly rushing from one uncompleted task to another. We have calendars and to-do lists and sub-lists on our to-do lists. We have reminders to do our to-do lists. We don't have to read books any more – we can pay for a service that reads them to us. That's great if you then lie on the couch and think about what you're hearing, but it's not so good if you're then surfing the Web and checking how many 'likes' your last social media post received.

Carl Honoré, author of *In Praise of Slow*, said in answer to the question 'Why do we live so fast today?' that: 'Speed is fun, sexy, an adrenaline rush. It's like a drug and we are addicted. At the same time, the world has become a giant buffet of things to do, consume, experience – and we rush to have it all. The modern workplace also pushes us to work faster and longer while technology encourages us to do everything faster and faster.'

Eckhart Tolle, author of *The Power of Now*, encourages us to realise that what's really important is in the here and now and not in the next moment, and that it's an illusion to think that what really matters is the next moment. It's not – life only consists of this moment and to realise the power of now.

The main obstacle to slowing down is the great social pressure to do more, more of the time. There are countless books on how to get more done in less time, in order that we can do more. Cities like New York are built on speed. If you've ever walked through Manhattan during the morning rush hour, you'll know exactly what I mean. You get run over if you stop.

Slowing down also means doing less and only doing one thing at a time. We need to learn to focus on one activity at a time and enjoy it. This means putting less on the to-do list, even creating a not-to-do list. Slowing down also means letting go, or delegating all of those activities that are neither urgent nor important.

Slowing down, if only for a few minutes, allows us to pause; to take a moment to think about what we're doing and where we're going. It allows us to reprioritise and focus on what matters most. It stops us wasting time. Slowing down actually allows us to achieve more in the long run.

Focus On Your Strengths

Doing less and doing one thing at a time requires us to focus on our signature strengths – those abilities that come naturally to us and that we love and enjoy doing. These are talents that create success for us. When we focus on these talents and turn them into strengths, it creates value for us in the marketplace. It differentiates us from others. We get known for what we bring to the team and the table, what results we'll create, regularly and repeatedly.

My friend Paul is a natural strategiser. He has the most profound ability to know which course of action needs to be taken at any given time. He's at his best when he's deciding what needs to be done in order to turn a vision into reality. Over the years he's learnt to focus all of his time and energy into building strategies for the companies he works for and helping others to do the same. As such, he's been very successful.

We need to learn to focus on these abilities. The Pareto principle, also commonly known as the 80/20 rule, states that 80 per cent of results come from only 20 per cent of our efforts. For example, 80 per cent of a business's profit will come from 20 per cent of its customers; 80 per cent of work is generally done by only 20 per cent of people; 80 per cent of our productivity comes from only 20 per cent of the work that we actually do.

We need to find and focus on that 20 per cent. When we do this, we'll achieve so much more for less. Less time, money and effort – all with much less stress. Imagine how much more time and energy you would have if you were able to eliminate over 80 per cent of your workload!

Most jobs consist of a limited number of activities that need be repeated on a regular basis. If that number was, for example, 10 regularly repeated tasks, then the Pareto principle indicates that 80 per cent of our effectiveness would come from just two of those tasks. It's staggering to think that nearly 80 per cent of what we do brings us limited returns or, to put it more succinctly, is a waste of time.

When working with clients I advocate that they should regularly take inventory of what they do at work and how that makes them feel. As I once saw Marcus Buckingham suggest, I invite them to undertake a 5- to 10-day exercise inventorying a typical working week. After regular activity that you undertake, you must pause afterwards and ask yourself, was this something that I looked forward to doing, enjoyed doing and left me feeling energised afterwards? If it was, then write that on a green Post-it note and place it in your journal or notebook. If it was something that you really did not look forward to doing, didn't enjoy and felt drained afterwards, then write that on a red Post-it note and place it in your journal or notebook. If the activity was neither energising nor draining, then write that on an orange Post-it note and place it in your journal or notebook.

After a week or so you will have created a traffic light of all of your typical workday activities and then you need to take a step back and look at how much of your time is spent focusing on your strengths. You need to let go of all the activities that are red, minimise the number of activities that are orange, and prioritise those that are green.

This exercise is not foolproof and requires negotiation and help from others, but it's a brilliant starting place to create more time by focusing on your strengths. I have taken a number of clients through this exercise and all were completely stunned by the results, especially how much time they were spending on activities that drained them and contributed little value to the bigger picture.

Accept Your Limitations

We all have limitations, ceilings and parameters which we have to work within. We intuitively know that we need to stay within these boundaries and that we can't keep going beyond our limitations before something breaks, but yet we keep pushing, keep borrowing and keep going into the red, getting further and further into debt, hoping that we'll get away with it, until something happens to show us that we can't.

In 2012 I was cycling to work when I really started to struggle. It felt like my legs had turned to lead. No matter how hard I tried I couldn't keep the bicycle going in a straight line. I kept crashing into the kerb before finally managing to get to work and falling over. I had suffered a mini-stroke. Over the next three weeks I had three more before finally having a full-blown stroke which paralysed me and put me in hospital.

As I lay in hospital trying to make sense of what had happened to me, I realised that I had finally reached, and tried to go beyond, my limitations and my body had said no. It simply couldn't take any more. Years of stress, unresolved anger and a ridiculously high workload had finally taken their toll. Thankfully, and some say miraculously, it only took a few days before I was well enough to go home, but it then took a further four years to fully recover – if that's ever truly possible.

We have mental limits – there is only so much information we can handle at any one time. There are only so many tasks and projects that we can successfully deal with at any given moment. Yet we're constantly taking on more than we can reasonably handle and process at any given time.

We have emotional limits – there is only so much that we can carry at any one time. How many people and problems can any one person take on, carry and handle at the same time?

We have spiritual limits – there is only so much time we can go without adequate relational connections, living with meaning and purpose before we find ourselves plateauing and turning towards anything that takes away our pain and boredom.

We also have physical limits – there is only so much our bodies can do without adequate food, sleep and rest to function at their best. When we don't take the time to give our bodies what they need we experience dis-ease, which often leads to disease.

The signs are there for others to see. They can see that we're stressed and anxious all the time. That we're constantly angry and agitated by the smallest of things. That we can flare up in an instant and will project our angst and take out frustrations on others, often those closest to us. They, and we, deserve better.

Learn to Say No

'No' is possibly the hardest word in our modern vocabulary – even more than sorry. Your boss asks if you can stay late, handle more responsibility, do more and more, and you want to say no but you say yes. A client calls and asks if you can get this done today. She knows it should normally take a week, but it's important to her and she really needs you to help her out, so you say yes. Your colleague's got an important family event and desperately needs a favour from you and asks you to complete a report, so you say yes. It goes on and on...

We say yes to things we don't want to do. We say yes to things that we haven't got the capacity to handle, but we hope that in doing them it will propel us towards the goals we're aiming for. Often our fear and insecurities are creating an internal script, driving our human operating system, which keeps us saying yes to things we don't want to do and no to the things we actually want. We know that we can't keep going like this – living with stress and anxiety – and that something needs to change.

Saying yes to more, often means we're then forced to

say no and go back on our promises to others, especially those we love the most. How many children have been told that a parent will take them somewhere, or do something with them, only to be told later that it can't happen? Then we hope that saying sorry will be enough to mend the growing rifts that our actions create. It is to begin with, but after a while those we love stop hearing it; all they hear is that nothing ever changes.

How do you learn to say no and not feel bad about it? I find that there are a few steps that have helped me over the years, both in responding to emails and in speaking directly to a person, and I believe they will help you too. It's all about saying no with confidence and clarity:

1. Name: Refer to the person by their name. It's the most important word to them, and it conveys respect. *Hi Jane,*
2. Appreciation: Thank them for thinking about you and giving you the opportunity to help them. *Thank you for thinking of me – it means a lot.*
3. Reason: Then the real key is just to say that 'I need to say no because…', and then keep your reason brief and sincere. If appropriate, signpost them to someone else or other resources. Never lie or feel embarrassed about why you're saying no. *I need to say no because*

I don't have the capacity at the moment. You might want to speak to Lisa – she loves this kind of work and might be able to help you.

4. Encouragement: Then encourage them in what they are doing. I hope that it goes well. *I've always thought that you would do well with this kind of thing.*

This gets easier with time and practice.

Ask For Help

John Donne said, 'No man is an island entire of itself.' His inference was that no one is truly self-sufficient; that everyone is dependant and must rely on others to both survive and thrive. If we want to succeed at the life we chose for ourselves, we will need the help of others.

At the beginning of the Bible, God said, 'It's not good for man to be alone.' God was offering mankind a blueprint for successful living. A modern translation might put it more like this: 'You'll want to try and do this on your own, but I wouldn't recommend it. That's not how you're wired to succeed. It's your ego getting in the way. You'll think you can get by, doing everything by yourself, but that's not the way it works. If you accept this and make the decision that you need help, then you'll come to appreciate that everyone has a gift, talent and creative energy that was put there to help you to achieve everything that you want and desire, and they will need your help too.'

I think one of the reasons for my stroke was my perpetual inability to ask for help. I was always frightened that it was a sign of weakness and I often felt a sense of shame that I wasn't able to do everything that others could. I was unable to accept that there were limits to what I was capable of doing and could get done. A high work ethic is one thing; fear of what others think is another. It drives you and you can't stop, always afraid that you are not enough. I think for many reading this, it's time to get off the merry-go-round and learn that it's okay to be you.

Whether that's asking for help at home, at work or in life, we need the help of others. A client of mine had launched her start-up and was really excited about the future, but after a few months things began to stall. Over coffee she told me that she was just exhausted from trying to do everything – build her website, do social media, cold-call, write articles and attend networking meetings. We explored what it was that only she could do and in this case it was casting vision. She realised that she needed to delegate as much as possible – but where do you start and who do you ask? The key is always to start where you are, use what you have and do what you can. She posted on Facebook that she was looking for help with her project and she recruited two friends who said they had been really keen to get involved but didn't know how. Then the three of them reached out to their contacts and soon a friend of a friend offered to help with a promo video. Once she shared that online she was then able to recruit two others to help with social media and marketing. In four months she had done more than in the whole of the last year.

What can you delegate? Which tasks have you been putting off? Who could help you with that? Start with something small and, before you know it, you'll be a regular team player. Now wouldn't that make God smile?

Action points

- Delegate a task to someone else.
- Say no to something you've been avoiding.
- Spend one day this week focusing on playing to your strengths.
- Ask a friend or colleague for help.
- Do one thing each day that brings you joy.

Having learnt to slow down we need to get out of our heads and get rid of the stress and anxiety created by overthinking.

CHAPTER 6

Step 2: Get Out of Your Head

When we're living on purpose, we are able to move with grace and an effortless flow. We are filled with a quiet confidence that we're on track and heading in the right direction. We're clear about what we want and secure in the knowledge that every step we take is moving us ever closer to our dreams. We know that even if we take a wrong turn, we're able to laugh, pick ourselves up, learn from our action and joyfully get going again.

When we're living on purpose, we are able to feel a deep sense of peace no matter what's happening to us, even when we're really busy, and especially when we're under pressure. We are able to feel continually centred even in the midst of the storms that rage in our lives. We know that no matter what happens, we can handle it.

When we're living on purpose, we are able to let go of the pain and regret of the past – the things we did and didn't do. We are able to consciously create positive intentions about our future knowing that anything and everything is possible. We are not worried about what others think.

Yet for many of us, our day-to-day reality is the opposite. Each day, week and month is filled with stress, anxiety and overthinking. We're constantly tired and have little energy. We're so busy worrying that we rarely take the time to enjoy what we're doing in the moment.

All of this brain fog is stopping us from experiencing the quality of life that's available to us, and we need to learn to get out of our heads and live more from our hearts – we need to learn to live on purpose.

Overthinking

Overthinking is a modern-day curse. Our minds are constantly on the go, with endless thoughts racing through our heads, twisting and turning, going around in circles. We worry incessantly about everything.

The root cause of overthinking is worry and the root cause of worry is fear – best described as false evidence (or expectations) appearing real. This type of fear comes from a mindset that expects the worse to happen, which can be debilitating, holding us back and preventing us from taking action towards our dreams.

We're worried about what people think, what might happen. We're constantly reading too much into situations: 'What did they mean by that?', 'Why didn't they say hello?', 'What did that email really mean?', 'Why hasn't that person replied on instant messenger when I can see that they've received my note?' When we're constantly overthinking, we're never fully present, especially being emotionally present with others

When we're worried and overthinking we're always seeking answers. We try to make the connection in our mind, desperately trying to find a narrative that explains what we think is happening. We want control and approval and safety and security. Our mind keeps turning over, trying to find a way to make it so. All of that overthinking creates a huge amount of brain fog.

Because we have an unclear and incomplete picture of who we really are and our value, we struggle to see and believe what's truly possible. As a result, we're drained and exhausted trying to meet the false and often unreasonable expectations of others.

Kirsten Corley, author of *But Before You Leave*, says that, 'The root of overthinking is just wanting people to accept you and be happy with you because you are still learning how to be happy and accept yourself.'

Worrying about the past or the future means losing the joy of today. In the Bible Job, the unlikely protagonist, cries out, 'What I have feared the most, has come about.' One of the most commonly used phrases in the Bible is 'fear not'. It teaches us that what we think about with feeling, we attract and move towards. Fear and worry, we are told, is having faith in a negative outcome. One of the core teachings of the Bible is that we become what we believe.

Anxiety

When we're consciously overthinking, it can lead to us having a picture in our mind that imagines that things are much worse than they actually are. That picture then becomes a movie which plays continuously in our waking and sleeping moments. Our perceived inability to do anything about it compounds the issue. All of this over-thinking puts us into a spin.

Anxiety is a feeling of unease. It's a sense of dread. It's feeling nervous. It's an inner turmoil. It's that feeling we have when we know we've done something wrong and now we have to face the consequences. It's also that feeling we have when we have to have a difficult conversation with someone. It's what we feel before going into stressful situations. It's the fear of losing our home or not being able to feed our children or pay our bills. It's how we feel when we're not able to do the things we need and want to do. It's also the feeling we have before doing anything for the first time, or something in public. It's the feeling we have before asking the prettiest person in the room to dance with us – especially if we believe that there's a risk they'll say no.

When we're anxious we can experience an increased heart rate, difficulty in breathing, a tightening around the chest area and feeling sick. Our legs may shake, our mouths might feel dry and we can sweat more than usual. In extreme cases of anxiety, we can hyperventilate and pass out. More often than not, anxiety create brain fog and with it the inability to think clearly, take care of ourselves and make empowered decisions.

Being anxious all or most of the time is where the real challenge lies. It can make us feel isolated and want to withdraw. We can often feel like we're not able to cope and can find it difficult to eat, sleep and relax. We want to avoid social engagements. Anxiety stops us believing in ourselves and what's possible for our lives and acting accordingly. Anxiety can be very debilitating.

Stress

Overthinking and anxiety create a picture in our mind that imagines that things are much worse than they actually are. When combined with our perceived inability to do anything about it, the issue is significantly compounded, which leads to stress.

Stress is the body's natural biological and psychological response to anything that requires a response, especially those that it perceives are harmful situations.

When we perceive a threat – say a car driving very fast towards us, swerving recklessly and then mounting the pavement – our body triggers the release of stress hormones, especially cortisol and adrenaline, in order to raise our heart rate and give us the immediate energy to deal with the situation. That perceived threat then triggers the fight, flight or freeze response. In this scenario most people would jump out of the way, some would freeze in blind panic not knowing what to do, while others would look to see who else was in danger and move quickly to help them.

When that car is racing towards us, or we hear a very loud noise, or someone appears very menacing, a sudden surge of energy from the release of adrenaline gives us the tools we need to survive. The challenge is that much of what we perceive as a threat isn't actually harmful, it's our mind telling us it is.

We worry about the exam we have to take, or why our boss suddenly wants to see us, or what our parents will think about our intentions, and as we move from a state of peace to one of anxiety, we trigger the body's natural stress response. This is useful when a car's racing towards us, but of no value whatsoever when we're not actually in danger.

The body's response to stress is normal and can be positive, keeping us alert and ready to avoid danger. But stress becomes abnormal and negative when we're continually experiencing perceived threats without gaps to rest. Excessive stress leads to distress and dis-ease, which leads to all kinds of problems.

For many of us we're experiencing such high levels of stress and anxiety that our adrenal glands are permanently switched on, pumping out cortisol 24/7, regardless of what's actually happening. Consequently, we're unable to sleep due to the high levels of stress hormones in our bodies. We toss and turn and keep waking up throughout the night, and we wake up still feeling tired and not refreshed. Our bodies ache all the time. We're tense, especially in our neck and head. Our digestive systems struggle to cope and as a result we're experiencing high levels of indigestion, acid reflux and gut problems.

Excess stress leads to negative coping strategies, such as staying up late, overeating, drinking to excess, addictions to sex, gambling or drugs. All of which leads to more anxiety and stress. It's a vicious cycle. The good news is that it's a cycle which can be broken.

At the simplest and most basic level, I have found that if we're able to regularly slow down and consciously breathe, even if only for a few minutes each day, we'll soon discover that the brain fog lifts, our minds become quieter, the previously unheard messages coming from our intuition become much clearer, brighter and more vibrant, and our confidence to act on these messages becomes incredibly stronger.

There's a lot at stake here. The world needs your passion, message and ideas. Overthinking, anxiety and stress cause us to get stuck in our heads. Learning how to accept the things you can't change, changing the things you can and being grateful even in the most challenging situations will accelerate you to a place of profound peace.

Acceptance

The Serenity Prayer by Reinhold Niebuhr begins with the incredible and powerful statement 'God grant me the serenity to accept the things I cannot change, courage to change the things I can, and wisdom to know the difference.'

This prayer, written sometime around or before 1934, quickly became adopted by Alcoholics Anonymous and other 12-Step programmes that realised the benefit it brought to its members through adherence to its universal truth: until we stop denying and accept the reality of our situation, we cannot change it.

We reject and deny the reality of a situation because we wish things were different. We wish we were taller, slimmer, richer and younger. We wish we lived in different countries and had different jobs. We wish we'd done things differently. We wish that whatever we're going through wasn't so.

We're often in denial about the reality of our situation and, until we accept and embrace the truth, we can't move on.

Susan Jeffers said we need to 'Feel the fear and do it anyway.' Accepting the reality of a situation allows us to let go of the negative emotion around it, which allows us to see things from a different perspective. Seeing things from a different perspective opens the door to new possibilities and ways of being.

We're frightened to accept the situation and how we feel about it because we fear that in doing so it makes it real. If we ignore it, then hopefully it will go away. Yet it's already real and it's already happening. Suppressing the emotion we're feeling about it won't help us and will eventually come out. Accepting the reality of a situation is the first step to taking responsibility for changing it.

After my final stroke, I lay in the hospital and realised that my body was broken. I had pushed it too far, ignoring all of the warning signs, being in total denial of what my doctor had been telling me for years – that if I didn't make big changes, I was at huge risk of a heart attack or stroke. Finally, I had to accept the reality of my situation. I couldn't talk, walk, eat or go to the toilet on my own. It was humiliating, but I knew that I couldn't ignore it any longer. While the nurses weren't looking, I rolled myself out of bed and dragged myself across the floor, using my good arm and leg to help me, made my way to the toilets and sat under the shower and washed myself. It was a start. After being released from hospital I attended all of my rehab sessions, sought nutritional advice and took my meds. I asked for help.

Stephen Covey said that the first habit of highly successful people is to be proactive – to accept responsibility for everything in your life and then choose your response accordingly. Raising awareness must lead to acceptance and responsibility. When we take responsibility for everything that's happening in our lives, we can then begin the journey to change it. And for all of the things that we believe we can't change, there are far more that we actually can.

Take Action

When we're stressed and anxious, we overthink. Thoughts keep buzzing around our mind, racing from one corner to another, each one creating more thoughts which in turn create others. At the heart of all this thinking is the belief that, somehow, we'll figure it all out through more thinking. That never happens – clarity always comes through action, not thinking.

We can nearly always do far more than we think we can. People are incredibly resourceful and will always find ways to get something done even when there appears to be no way. When we're stressed and anxious and don't think we can change our situation, we need to tap into our inner resourcefulness and take inspired action.

Action nearly always means asking for something: time, talent or resources. When we need something it inevitably means having to do something that takes us outside of our comfort zone. That and a fear of rejection cause us not to want to ask for help, and as a result we miss out on the joy that comes from having our request granted. Learning not to fear the word 'no' will propel us to new heights of success. If you don't ask you won't get. Those who ask often enough, will eventually receive.

There are also times when we don't know whether to accept what's happening to us or know if it's even possible to change the circumstances of our life. At times like these we need another strategy.

Gratitude

There are many times in our lives when we want more than we're experiencing: more love, money, happiness and opportunity. There are also times in our lives when we want the pain of our situation to go away. The key to both situations is the practice of gratitude.

Being grateful for what we already have in our lives opens the door for more. As we've seen, what we think about with feeling we attract and move towards. It's easy to be grateful when things are going well. The challenge is to be grateful when things are going badly.

A client came to me deeply frustrated with her job. She had originally joined an NGO working with people with complex problems. No two days were the same. She loved it but, over the years, the organisation grew and her role changed from working less with people and more with paperwork. She got to the point where she couldn't face going into work each day. She said that she didn't really want to change companies and had asked on several occasions for her role to be changed, but had been told that it wasn't possible.

She didn't know what to do. I asked her what she could be grateful for and she instantly replied, 'Nothing.' But after a few minutes' silence, she began to list all of the people she was grateful for. She quickly moved towards being grateful for all of the material blessings she had, her health and her family. She was eventually able to start giving thanks and feeling grateful for her job – the fact that she had one and that it was secure – and that she was valued and appreciated.

Every day when she went to work, she practised giving thanks and being grateful for her job. Even though it frustrated her, she looked for things she could feel grateful for. A few weeks later the stress and anxiety she had been feeling about her job began to melt away. She was happy to be there. She even said to me that if nothing changed, she was okay with that. About six weeks later, her manager asked her if she would like to take on a different role working with the organisation's customers. That role brought her into daily direct contact with people and allowed her to enjoy the interactions she craved so much.

Gratitude is an emotion and what we think about with feeling we move towards. My client had been locked in a cycle of thinking negatively about her work situation which caused the negativity to increase. Once she began to think and feel a positive emotion around her situation – being grateful – it had to change.

Does that mean we should feel grateful for the tragedies in our lives, such as death and sickness? I don't think that would be healthy or wise. We can, however, find things that we can be grateful for in those dark and difficult times. When we're sick, we can be grateful for those parts of us that are functioning well. When a loved one dies, we can be grateful for their life and impact. In anything and in everything we can find something to be grateful for.

Being grateful keeps us grounded in the present moment, which is key for experiencing joy, peace and happiness. Being grateful makes us more agreeable and open to others. It helps connect us to something much larger than ourselves. Every religion stresses the importance of being thankful and grateful. Gratitude helps us to release strong emotions which keep us from manifesting our intentions.

Gratitude decreases stress; if we're grateful for something we're not likely to be stressed or anxious about it. It reduces depression. It increases our happiness and life satisfaction. It improves our health and relationships. It has shown to heal childhood wounds and remove limiting beliefs. It is a form of mindfulness as it causes us to stop and reflect. As we practise gratitude it releases more positive emotions which help us to feel more alive and sleep better, all of which improves our immune system.

When we regularly feel grateful for what we have in our lives it causes us to want less. We no longer feel the internal drive to want more and consume more. The paradox is that even though we want less we receive more – what we think about with feeling increases.

Taking the time to develop a daily habit of journaling, writing down all that you're happy about and grateful for, will transform your life more than you could ever imagine. Each day take a few minutes to take some deep breaths, feel grateful for everything in your life, visualise your intentions and let go of any negative emotions around them. Do that and you will experience profound levels of happiness, joy and peace, as well as live an abundant life.

Action points
- Consider what you are grateful for this week.
- Write in your journal.

- Accept the truth about a situation.
- Change something you're not happy about.
- Take time out to embrace the joys of today.

Having got out of our head we need to now get into our hearts, and the way to do that is to remember who we are.

CHAPTER 7

Step 3: Remember Who You Are

We are born without limitations and get to choose how we live, how we spend our waking hours and the work that we choose to do. We get to choose what we think about, what we believe is possible and what's important. We get to choose and define our life's purpose and goals for ourselves, and the activities we want to engage in to bring that about. We have the inalienable right to determine the course of our life and have been given the power to bring that about. No one has the right to tell us what dreams we can and can't choose for ourselves, not even God. If it's legal, ethical and fair, you can dream it, and if you can dream it, you can do it.

We are born as effortless creators. We are born with the capacity to create anything that we want. We are worthy of having big dreams. Intention is a crystal clear mental picture combined with the belief that it is possible and that it will happen because we are worthy of any dream that we choose. Often we forget this and, when the pursuit of our dreams becomes slow and laborious, it's usually a sign that we've forgotten who we really are. Once we remember and focus once again on what we really want (our heart) we are then only one positive intention away from living the abundant life. Through the power of intention we have the ability to create our own future; to bring about what we want and desire, and to help others do the same. Infinite possibilities are available to us at any time – everything we dream and desire is only an intention away.

Intentions are created through the imagination. Either instantly or over the course of time, we build up in our mind a clear mental picture of what we want: a picture of radiant physical health; a picture of us graduating from the university of our choice; a picture of us doing the work that we love and most want to do; a picture of us living in a certain type of house or driving a certain type of car; a picture of us writing a book or solving a global problem. Regardless of what the picture is, two truths exist:

1. You get to choose what it is that you want.
2. What you think about with feeling, you will attract and bring about.

We live in, and are coheirs to, a world of infinite possibilities. We plant a seed in the ground and the earth, with its infinite power and possibilities, incubates that seed and in time brings about a harvest.

This is the same with the power of intention – the power of infinite possibilities. What you imagine and think about with feeling becomes an intention. That intention is like a seed planted into the realm of infinite possibilities. When that seed is watered with the belief and expectation that it will happen, it produces a harvest. Like seeds, all intentions – both positive and negative – are treated equally in the realm of infinite possibilities. You attract what you think, and you become what you believe. Most of us live our lives way below our creative potential or are creating limited realities because of what we believe is possible.

We are not born with any limiting concepts of who we are or what we are able to achieve. We don't know what race or gender we are. We are free of class and social mobility restrictions. We live contentedly in the present moment not worried about the future. We are born with a natural understanding that in order to receive we first have to ask, so we cry when we're hungry and our carer feeds us.

Our minds, like sponges, begin to readily accept the seeds of both possibility and limitation that the influences we explored in Chapter 3, such as our experiences and families of origin, begin to teach us. The baby that wants comfort quickly learns not to cry out for help if no one comes, deciding that it's better not to ask than to ask and be disappointed.

Our parents project on to us their own perception of reality, including the limitations that they were told and chose to believe. Our education systems shape our conscious reality of how the world works, and our communities tell us what they believe is possible and permissible. The mind, like the soil, accepts what it is given and works to increase that which it's given. Positive or negative, you reap what you sow.

Experiences Shape Our Reality

I vividly remember my first day at school like it was only yesterday. My mother dropped me off at the front gate where, along with all the other new students, we were welcomed and then taken to our classroom. I remember feeling so sad, confused and incredibly lonely. I felt abandoned. As a child I failed to understand that my mother was also feeling horrible and would cry all day herself, as I then did when I took my own children to school for the first time.

We were taken into a changing area to hang up our coats when another student, looking at the colour of my skin, said to me, 'You look like a poo,' and some of the other children laughed at me. I was shocked by what he said. Feelings of self-doubt and confusion overwhelmed me. I desperately tried to make sense of what was happening to me.

Our minds look for connections and we create stories that try to explain what we see and feel. The trouble is, very often those stories are false realities appearing true.

Jia Jiang, author of *Rejection Proof*, tells of a similar incident at his school. When he was a young boy, a well-meaning teacher created an exercise where students were given a gift after they said something positive about a fellow student, which went really well, except no one said anything about Jiang. Not a single student offered a word of encouragement or praise. He was left standing at the front of the class while the teacher tried every trick to get the students to say something. I imagine the silence was deafening.

Jiang said in his book that moment could have crushed him, but, somehow, he didn't allow that to happen. He made a decision to do something big with his life, to do something to show them all that they were wrong. It became a driving force that motivated him forward in life. When he gave his TED Talk – 'What I learned from 100 days of rejection' – he did exactly that.

Unlike Jiang, my mind failed to see the full picture of what was happening to me. In that moment my mind sought to connect the two experiences of that morning and find a story that made sense of it. My mind chose to offer me a story, which I readily accepted and believed, that I had been rejected by both my mother and my classmates because there was something wrong with me and that I wasn't good enough.

When we create these stories, our minds look for evidence to back them up and my mind brought back to me all of the previous experiences in my life that would confirm what I was thinking. With each memory the story grew stronger. Running out of memories, my mind then sought to look for external evidence and, with every encounter, I would begin to read into it things that just weren't there. Eventually that story became a belief that controlled every area of my life.

If you think that there's something wrong with you and that you're not good enough, your world contracts. You no longer see a world of infinite possibilities but a world of limitations. You believe for less, ask for less and settle for less. With each subsequent thought and decision your world becomes smaller and you learn to become comfortable in that world. You hang out with others living in that contracted world and together it becomes normal and you learn to survive.

That belief negatively affected me for over 40 years until I eventually saw myself for who I really was and began to let go of all of the negative emotion. I was living a false reality. As previously described, fear is false evidence appearing real or false expectations (of others) appearing real, and, as far as I'm concerned, fear can go to hell and shame can go there too.

Test your assumptions

We often create a hypothesis in our minds; we believe that something is true – that something can't or will happen. Yet how do we know that it is actually true?

Byron Katie, in her book *Loving What Is*, asks people four questions:

1. 'Is it true?'
2. 'Can you absolutely know it's true?'
3. 'How do you react, what happens, when you believe that thought?'
4. 'Who would you be without that thought?'

She then invites readers to explore what she calls a

'turnaround', to find a statement that better reflects the truth of the situation. When her readers do this, they find that false and limiting beliefs are replaced by truth, and truth will always set you free.

A client of mine only had three days of paid leave left available to him and was not prepared to ask his employer for the additional two days he required to go to a conference in the USA because he was convinced that they would say no. Deep down he wasn't prepared to handle the rejection and perceived shame of failing if they said no.

I asked him 'Is it true?' He answered truthfully, 'I don't know.' I then invited him to build a mental picture of what he really wanted and, once he had that, to ask his employers for what he wanted, knowing that all they could do was say no. Rejection, if it came, would be to his request for time off, with a reason, and most certainly would not be a rejection of him as a person.

He asked his manager who said yes in principle but referred him to the HR department for the final decision. They seemed really excited about the conference and not only granted his request but paid for his conference ticket believing it to be of use in his work and therefore of benefit to the company. He had been stressed and anxious about this for weeks, with his mind constantly overthinking the situation. When he took action all of that stress simply vanished.

How many times are we convinced that things are true and can't be changed? The key is to get out of our heads and into our feet by taking action. We nearly always believe that our ideas will work. However, it's only when we act on those ideas that we get instant feedback as to whether we're right and on track, or wrong and need to adjust.

Another client had been repeatedly assigned the early shift at work, needing to be there by 05:45. Initially she didn't mind, but over the weeks found herself increasingly put out by what she considered were unreasonable demands by her manager.

She was convinced that he had it in for her but when asked 'Is it true?' quickly moved to thinking that he chose her because she always turned up on time and was never late – which she thought was unfairly rewarding the unreliable people by allowing them to lie in each day. Her mind kept going around in circles. She then thought it was because she was being punished for having been sick and needing time off earlier in the year. Her mind was racing, desperately trying to find the correct mental connection to her conundrum.

I encouraged her to take action and ask for her shifts to

be changed. She said she was terrified of doing it, wanting to avoid conflict and fearful that her boss might say no. She failed to take action, nothing changed and her misery continued.

Let Go of Fear

Fear is anything negative that you believe, or expect, will happen.

When we struggle with doubt and worry, or are plagued by fear, we diminish, and it eventually cancels out our positive intentions. We want a career that allows us to bring all of us to what we do, to follow our passions and to make a difference, but we don't believe it's possible – after all, nobody in our family has ever done this. Because we don't believe it's possible or that we deserve it, so it becomes impossible and doesn't happen.

Intentions always need to be married to positive expectations. We need to be like children writing letters to Father Christmas asking for all of the toys we want and desire, believing without any doubt that we will get them. We need to believe that what we want is possible, that we deserve it and expect it to happen.

I often imagine that there is a storehouse in heaven dedicated to fulfilling our requests and intentions. Every prayer, thought and intention is a signal emanating from us directly to heaven like a lighthouse brightly shining on the darkest of nights. When that intention is clear and bright and is combined with positive expectations, that signal goes all the way to heaven and is seen by the fulfilment angels and, at once, they joyfully grant us our desires. Each intention is stamped with a huge red 'APPROVED' and shipped straight out of the door.

However, when our intentions are mixed with fear and doubt that signal becomes blurred and unclear. It doesn't reach heaven and, for those rare signals that do, the angels are unclear as to what we want and therefore don't know what to do. They don't play guessing games, so they have no alternative but to leave it unanswered until the signal becomes clearer. Their hands are tied. No clear picture, no answer. That's the way it is and will always be. They often despair knowing the infinite possibilities that are available to us and the simple mechanism required to unlock them – remembering who we are.

The key to unlocking the infinite possibilities available to us is twofold. Firstly, we need a fresh revelation of who we are, the world and our rightful place in it. Secondly, we then need to let go of the fear – the false evidence appearing real and the negative emotion.

We don't have to struggle to let go of limiting beliefs. All we need to do is see, hear and experience truth. When we know and accept the truth, it will set us free and replace the lies, limiting beliefs and fear that so easily entangle us and hold us back. When we operate from a place of truth we reconnect to infinite possibilities.

Remember Who You Are: Seven Truths Heaven Wants You to Know

1. You are not a mistake

Before the creation of the world, God saw a time in the future when a group of people would cry out for His help, asking Him to take away their pain, to ease their struggle and to resolve their situation. They would be overwhelmed with problems that they couldn't solve, some of them so big that common wisdom said that nothing could be done. God knew differently. He knew that these problems, vast in their number and complexity, each required a huge level of passion, ability, commitment and creativity to sort out. So He created you.

God in His infinite wisdom chose you. He created you as His solution to those problems. He created you as His intention and He said, 'Let there be and there was.' There was no fear or doubt in His mind, no hesitation or concern. He never changed or wanted to change His mind. As each day passed, He grew in eager expectation, waiting with held breath for that time when you would appear.

He positioned you at a specific time in history and uniquely placed you in geography and community, designed to shape and prepare you for the work that you were meant to do. He built the universe around you to support you in everything that you set your mind to do and, like every good father, when He looks at you, He smiles and sings with joy. He is not angry with you and He is not disappointed in you. He declares that you are perfect. There is nothing wrong with you and He wants nothing from you in return. Like the very best of fathers, all He longs for is to see His children happy and healthy – and maybe visit Him once in a while.

2. You are fearfully and wonderfully made

Everything about you boldly proclaims that you are a unique masterpiece, a one-off creation, a limited edition that will never be repeated. When they made you, they threw away the mould.

Your unique fingerprints, retina, DNA and talents proudly state that there is no one like you. Out of the billions of people alive today there is no one exactly like you. Nor has there been or ever will be. There is no reusing or upcycling of disused parts. That's powerful. When we learn to accept the truth of our uniqueness and the value it bestows upon us, it empowers and releases us to accept our rightful place, step on to the stage prepared for us and shine brightly, very brightly. If there is only one of us, it means that we are special and valuable. Not better than anybody else, but equal to everyone else.

We don't ever have to look at anybody else and wish that we were more like them. We don't have to look in the mirror and wish that our favourite celebrity was looking back at us; that we had become them.

When we look in the mirror, we see a reflection that is badly distorted by the socially constructed ideas of beauty and value. We have been taught that those who are beautiful are of more value than those who are not. We have been taught that those who are slimmer are more attractive than those who are not. We have come to believe that those who make the most money are of greatest value to society and that we should do everything to emulate them... except that's a road to stress, anxiety, unhappiness and depression.

Comparing ourselves to others leads to unhappiness. If we do that, we'll never feel that we are enough or have enough. Somebody will always have more and therefore be more. We'll strive to keep up, even when we can't. Looking at how others look and how they lead their lives will cause us to despair and feel despondent. When we understand that our true value is not found in what we look like, what we do or how much we earn, but is found in God and who He says we are, we can begin to let go of the lies we've believed about ourselves and walk into the realm of infinite possibilities and enjoy all that it holds for us.

3. You are talented beyond measure

You have a gift, a talent so profound in its ability that nobody else can do what you do in the way that you do it. The talents you have are directly linked to the work that you are meant to do. You already have all the talent, drive and creative ability you will ever need.

Some have a strong driving talent that shapes all that they think and do – it's an ability to do a particular type of work, going to ever deeper levels of proficiency. Others have two strong talents that blend with each other that lead to particular vocational fields, while others have multiple talents that allow them to do many things.

Some have the ability to work with information. Others prefer the world of people and ideas. Some excel using their hands to work with objects. Others love to use their entire body. Each talent also brings with it a particular ability to solve certain types of problems, for example intellectual, spiritual, psychological, administrative, emotional, physical and creative issues.

All of your quirkiness, passion and creativity are given to you to enjoy. There is no greater feeling than to be so deeply engaged in what you do that time stands still. Passion is the God-given desire to give your time, talent and energy to whatever matters most. Your drive to be with certain types of people, to solve specific problems, to study distinct subjects and learn various skills are all coming from within. This is the desire to bring all of you to what you do.

Aligning your talents with your passions and callings is essential to living a life full of meaning, purpose, connection and contribution.

4. The world needs your passion, ideas and message

Right now, somebody somewhere is crying out for that thing which only you can do. I can't do what you can do, and you can't do what I can do. It doesn't matter how unusual or niche your abilities are, somebody somewhere needs your talent, passion and creativity.

That dream you've had for years about the workshop you want to deliver, the book that you are born to write, the talk you want to give, the business you want to launch, and even that small side hustle you want to do on evenings and weekends, that passion is God-given and designed to point you in the direction you're meant to go. No matter what it is, somebody somewhere needs what you can offer and will almost certainly pay you for it. These things don't have to be big or clever, deeply spiritual or profitable. If that desire burns within you, you need to follow it. Learning to hear what your intuition is saying will always provide you with all that you need and support you to get going.

It's essential that you do your thing. Nobody benefits if you try to be like everybody else or try to sound exactly like every other message, repeating what everybody else is saying. This is the time for you to step out of the shadows – often somebody else's shadow –do your thing and shine. The world needs your passion.

We're so frightened to stand up for what we believe in, worried that we'll be judged and rejected, but in doing so we're rejecting ourselves first. We never give others a chance to say yes to our talent, knowledge and ideas. If we don't do that which we're meant to do, that means a lot of the world's problems will go unanswered for a time.

Make no mistake though – God is always looking for that one person He can elevate to a place where He can move through them. Searching for that woman, man or child who will dare to say yes and follow their passion. God is always looking to bring the entire resources of heaven to support those who are brave.

You were born for such a time as this. The world has been waiting in eager anticipation for you to come into a full revelation of who you are, so that you can confidently and unashamedly bring your talent, passion and message to those who need it.

5. Your past doesn't equal your future

No matter what you've done or think you've done or have failed to do, God says that you are qualified to receive the life you most want to live and do the work that you love and are meant to do. All of the resources of heaven are available to you. You do not have to do anything to earn this favour. You have it because you are His child and He loves you. You don't have to give anything to enjoy this favour – not your time, talent or money; you just have to freely receive it.

We erroneously believe that we're somehow disqualified by what we've done; that our mistakes will haunt us. If we're going to live the life that's available to us, we need to let go of our mistakes and learn to accept ourselves, warts and all.

God takes all of our mistakes – intentional or accidental – locks them in a box, stamps 'Forgiven and Forgotten' on the box and throws away the key. To ensure that they can never be used against us by anyone else, He then wraps a huge chain around the box and throws it into the deepest seas. The trouble is that we like to go fishing. We're always searching for reasons to believe that we're not good enough, haven't done enough and need to do more. We want to hold on to our past failures and indiscretions believing that they somehow disqualify us from having all that we want. They don't and it's time to let them go.

Your past doesn't equal your future. No matter where you've come from or the path you've taken to get here, you are only one intention away from creating the life that you want. One single intention is all it takes.

6. You become what you believe

Our past doesn't determine our future, but our thoughts do. We attract what we think of and become what we believe. If you think that's it's possible it will become possible for you. If you think that it's not possible then it will become impossible for you.

Brian Tracy would often say that you become like the five people you hang around with the most. Their beliefs become your beliefs; their actions soon enough become yours. The key, therefore, is to intentionally cultivate relationships with people who have achieved what you want to achieve and who are on the same journey. It never pays to be the smartest or richest person in the room.

We need to question our beliefs. We need to challenge the assertions and assumptions we make about ourselves, the world and our place in it. How do you know you can't do something? In the words of The Beautiful South, 'How do you know you can't swim, until you have drowned?'

We give up too quickly on our dreams, because we don't believe that they are possible. We reject ourselves because we don't believe that we are qualified or good enough. Let others reject you if they don't like your ideas or your version of reality, but please never reject yourself. You are here for a reason and the world needs your passion, message and ideas. Keep going until your reality matches that of your intentions. It will. It has to.

7. You were born for such a time as this

No matter what you are dreaming for, the perfect time to

start to make that happen is now.

When we think about our dream, we inevitably begin to wonder how it can happen and what we have to do to make it happen. We look at our skills, knowledge, contacts and bank balance and quickly conclude that it could never happen. When we do this, our strong and clear intention is no longer infused with a positive expectation and it begins to fade. As a result, heaven's vault remains closed.

When we set an intention, there is often, if not always, something we need to do to align ourselves with the people and resources that we'll need and that means taking inspired action – action prompted through our intuition, free from stress and striving. Doing this requires that we tap into our inner resourcefulness, which is always greater than external resources. Resources ebb and flow like the tide, while resourcefulness is infinite and can be nurtured and developed. There are countless stories of people who made their first million only to lose it and then quickly make their second, often much more because of what they learnt and who they became in the process.

You can only start from where you are right now. You need to stop worrying that you've missed your opportunity, that it's too late. You might only have limited education, few resources and no rich and famous people to call, but you can use what you have right now. In putting what you have to good use, you begin to tap into the universal law of sowing and reaping. As you sow the little you have, you will reap much more. You need to do what you can. There is no other way. You can't do any more than that, but you must do that. You can make that call, write that letter or send that email. You can begin to write that blog, make that video and ask others to join and help you.

Not only must we start small, we must also not despise the day of small beginnings. Everyone starts off where they are, using what they have and doing what they can. Every global brand was once a start-up. I think so many people in later years are put off starting something new because they feel that others will look down on them, negatively believing that they should have achieved more by now. We need to prove ourselves faithful in the small things and, in turn, we will be rewarded with much more.

Take the time each day to focus on your intention. Let go of any anxiety and quietly listen to what your intuition says to you about what inspired action you need to take. Dare to do it and let the magic happen.

Action points

- Set intentions for your life, work and happiness.
- Regularly let go of physical anxiety.
- Ask yourself 'Is it true?'
- Think on the seven truths that heaven wants you to know.
- Reach out to someone that you would like in your life.
- Listen and act on your intuition.

In the next chapter we'll look at the how letting go of the past opens the door to infinite possibilities.

CHAPTER 8

Step 4: Let Go of the Past

There are many times in our lives when we set a very clear intention fuelled with the expectation that we will receive it – but we don't. We affirm our intention and declare that we are worthy and that what we want is on its way. We journal, create vision boards and practise gratitude, but something's not working. We're not sure what that something is. We buy more books, we watch videos, we take on board what people are teaching, and we do what they say – but still we don't see the full manifestation of what we're dreaming for.

In the book *The Secret*, the author quotes from a well-known passage in the Bible, where Jesus says in Mark 11:24, 'Whatever you ask for in prayer, believe that you have received it and it will be yours.' The process is codified into three steps: ask, believe, receive.

However, that passage in the Bible contains one further sentence which is crucial to know if we are to become the person that we were born to be and live the life that we know is freely available to us. That sentence is in verse 25: 'And when you stand there praying, if you hold anything against anyone forgive them.'

Forgiveness is the essential and often forgotten key to experiencing all that life has to offer. And, like all spiritual principles, it works 24/7 whether we are conscious of it or not, and whether we like it or not. Not forgiving, or 'unforgiveness', is simply holding on to negative emotions.

When we hold on to negative emotions, they become blocks that prevent us from successfully manifesting our intention. That bright, crystal-clear intention that should shine like a powerful beam in order to attract what we want, becomes dull and subdued. Like a torch with old batteries, it fails to light our path and we can't see where we're going any more. Far from illuminating that path it becomes a stumbling block, even dangerous. I believe that holding on to negative emotions negates our intention. It's that serious. We need to learn to let go of them if we're going to achieve all that we set our mind towards.

When we are young, we tend to worry about the things we've done, the choices we made. When we're older we tend to worry far more about the things we didn't do, the decisions we failed to make and the opportunities we didn't seize, rather than the things we have done. We keep thinking about what we should have done differently: 'If only I'd done this or that.' The past is exactly that – it's passed, it's gone and can't be recovered or changed – yet we visit it daily in our minds, always hoping to change it, to make it somehow different.

The movie of our past plays in our mind; we change the characters and rewrite the plot, but when we open our eyes, nothing has changed, it's still the same. We need to learn to accept our past, change our internal narrative around the events and let go of the angst. Negative emotion rarely serves anyone.

We worry about the future. Will we have enough money? Will we find the person of our dreams? Will we be happy? We worry about things that might happen. We worry about things that might not happen. We're often stuck in an endless loop of analysis paralysis. It's the 'yes but, no but' syndrome. We're so very often waiting for something to go wrong. We need to let go of the worry.

As we go through life, we also experience events – moments that we create or that happen to us – that affect us. In those moments we experience either positive or negative emotions. Someone tells us that we're no good and, in that moment, we feel a rush of negative emotion flood our body. Our heart rate increases, our breaths get shorter, and we might feel anger and resentment, shame and guilt, or that we're not good enough. The emotions we feel in that moment are real, very real.

We are born with the natural ability to let go of the emotions that we feel. We're supposed to feel them and then let them go. We see that in children. A child falls over and, in that moment, feels a whole raft of emotions. She looks around and her loving parents smile and say 'Oops' and laugh and the child lets go of the negative emotion, smiles and gets up and tries to walk again. That same child bangs her knee and is in real pain and is crying, but Mum kisses it better and she immediately lets go of the negative emotion.

As adults we learn to hold on to those emotions. We come to the realisation that kissing it better no longer works and that the anger, shame and guilt we feel as a result of our actions are very powerful and deeply affect us.

When we hold on to these emotions it's like we're holding on to our breath. Someone says something to affect us or something negative happens to us and, in that moment, we experience a sharp intake of breath and metaphorically we hold on to it, never breathing out and therefore never letting it go.

Emotion is energy in motion and that breath – that emotion – gets stuck. It gets trapped somewhere in the body. Initially it feels very uncomfortable but, in time, we get used to it. It often becomes a familiar friend. We can get so used to it that we no longer experience the emotion, but we *become* the emotion. We no longer say, 'I'm feeling angry, sad or confused' but instead say 'I am angry, I am sad and I am confused.' Every time we say it, it becomes like a self-fulfilling prophecy that gets truer with every utterance. And what we think about with feeling, we attract and expand.

Often when we experience traumatic events we hold on to that negative emotion for years, possibly for the rest of our lives. And in doing so we often become stunted; we fail to grow emotionally and spiritually, failing to reach our full potential. It's like in the film *Sliding Doors*, when the character fails to get on the train and, in that moment, they become two people – the imaginary one living the life she was supposed to lead and the other living a limited life. I've seen this happen many times in my own life and in the lives of those I've worked with. Something happened to them and they held on to the emotion around the event, struggling to let it go and, as a result, always lived a life less lived. It's a high price to pay.

When we experience negative emotions, we tend to either suppress them or express them. Both can be appropriate, but at the same time very destructive.

Suppressing Emotions

When we suppress our emotions, what we are trying to do is avoid experiencing them. We try hard to avoid the feeling, preferring instead to swallow them in an attempt to get rid of them as fast as possible. We also suppress our emotions because we don't know how best to communicate what we want, or we feel that we are not able to.

Negative emotions are the body's way of communicating to us that something is wrong and that we need to take remedial action. Emotions such as pain, anger and fear are all signals from the body that something is potentially wrong and that we need to deal with it. Suppressing these emotions is very harmful.

When someone says something derogatory towards us, we feel anger and contempt towards that person and what they said. In this case, that anger we're feeling is the body's way of communicating to us that something about that person is toxic and harmful to us, and that we need to extricate ourselves.

It's also the body's way of communicating to us that what this person is saying is not true. If we keep holding on to what they say and the feelings that it brings up in us, the brain will look for evidence from our past to help us confirm what they have said. Once confirmed, it becomes part of our human operating system.

That anger is a gift from our body designed to force us to stop and think, to assess the situation and respond accordingly. In this case to reject what the other person is saying. In between every event (or stimulus), there is always a gap before our response. That gap might only be a fraction of a microsecond, but it is always there. Recognising this, we can learn to live in that gap and choose to respond rather than react. Anger management courses wisely advocate counting to 10 before responding.

The fear we experience as a response to what's happening around us is the body wanting us to know that something is wrong and that we need to do something about it quickly. If we suppress that fear, not only can it be dangerous to us in the immediate moment, but very harmful to us in the long term as that fear becomes a part of us, and we then avoid people and situations that we know trigger it. In short, we become fearful people.

Cassie was confronted by a dog that growled at her in the woods when she was young. Ever since she has had a terrible fear of dogs that prevents her from going anywhere or doing anything that might bring her into contact with dogs. That once natural and appropriate fear has taken over her life and she is now a fearful person.

Suppressing negative emotions causes them to get stuck. We learn to live with the emotion but eventually the body wants to get rid of it and the message changes from discomfort to dis-ease, and then eventually to depression and disease.

Suppressed negative emotions will always come out eventually.

Expressing Emotions

The second way to deal with negative emotions is to express them, either in the moment or after the event.

In that same event when somebody says something derogatory to us, we feel anger and contempt towards that person and, instead of suppressing it or letting it go, we express it, often loudly and sometimes violently. We scream and shout, we fight back verbally, we throw things and we hit back physically.

Expressing our emotions can be a very positive thing, but again only when we practise living in the gap between the stimulus and the response. In that gap we are able to choose the most appropriate response, deciding whether to express that anger verbally or physically or to walk away.

Not finding a way to live in the gap, to learn to take a moment to choose our response, often means we end up reacting rather than responding. Reacting tends to be forceful, angry and accusatory. We lash out and say things that we later regret. We cause damage to ourselves and those around us. We cause people to avoid us and our world contracts.

We can react in the moment and both express and suppress our emotions at the same time: we feel the shame and pain of someone's words and, in that moment, we partially express some emotions and, at the same time, suppress different ones.

Those suppressed emotions will then seek an outlet. The body wants to let them go and often they come out through anger and frustration, which we then project on to others. The same words that others used on us, we now use on others. The treatment we received from others, we now meet out on others. It's a vicious cycle.

The third way of dealing with emotions is to just let them go.

Letting Go Of Emotions

All of us are born with the innate ability to feel negative

emotions and let go of them. We don't have to suppress them or express them if we choose not to. Instead we can feel the emotion in all its fullness, and then choose to let it go.

In order to let negative emotions go, we first need to feel them, to allow them to be present and to sit with them for a while, but we're often scared to do this. We don't want to fully feel the power of an emotion or allow it to fill us from head to toe. Emotions are powerful and we are afraid of them. We fear that if we really feel the full force of an emotion it has the power to overtake and consume us, and we'll get hurt – over and over again. We'll therefore do anything and everything in our power to avoid that.

So many of us have been hurt by love. We experienced such deep emotions and opened up our hearts to receive love, only to be let down, get hurt and be crushed. The pain and hurt we felt were so real that we want to avoid experiencing that ever again. As a result, we're fearful of opening up our heart to anyone else. What we desire the most is the thing we avoid the most because of the potential to get hurt again. We crave love but we fear pain and so we avoid love.

Many of us have been affected by grief; we have lost a loved one and it hurts. The feelings associated with grief are so deep and powerful that they can become terrifying.

In that split moment we think of our loved one and we are overwhelmed with the strongest emotions we have ever experienced, and it hurts. We struggle to breathe. Our eyes well up with tears. We sob uncontrollably, and feel such a depth of pain in our stomachs that we double over. We want it to end. We want it to be over so quickly that we do our best to suppress those feelings, to choke them back, swallow them and push them so far and deep down within us, never to be seen again. But that grief keeps coming back. The body tries its best to communicate to you that you need to do something.

In ancient cultures families and communities come together for a full seven days to wail and cry and fully feel and experience the full force of that grief. To allow it to do its work. After seven days they celebrate the life of their loved one and then get up and get on with life. Grief has done its work – it has cleared the body of all the hurt and unfulfilled hope. It has cleared out the fear and anger and, in doing so, has shifted all of the other emotions stuck in the body surrounding that person. Grief is powerful and transformational if you're prepared to feel it fully.

Being prepared to experience the fullness of an emotion is part of the process of letting it go and the main reason why we don't want to. Fully experiencing an emotion doesn't have to be something we need to be afraid of. We don't need to fear getting hurt or getting lost in the process. We can feel the emotion, be present with it, listen to the message it wants to offer us, and then, when we're ready, simply let it go.

Unforgiveness is holding on to negative emotions that we're unprepared or unwilling to let go of. We all need to relearn how to let go.

Learning to forgive ourselves and others

We have hurt ourselves as much as others have. At times we have been our biggest critic and worst enemy. We have said things about ourselves that others would get prosecuted for saying. We have treated ourselves in ways that we wouldn't treat an animal. We are angry and frustrated at ourselves for the things we've done and the things that we didn't do. We are complicated people.

We blame ourselves for our lot in life. If only we didn't marry that person. If only we hadn't taken that job or applied for that credit card. If only we'd done things differently. As we think on these things, a vortex of emotions sweeps through our minds and bodies, crushing our hopes and dreams, stamping on our spirit and taking us ever further away from our true potential and a life of infinite possibilities.

We blame others and often rightly so. Other people have treated us awfully. They have said things and done things to us that are inexcusable. We have been treated like punching bags by others who have sought to take out their insecurities and inadequacies on us. They have projected their angst on to us and we have suffered greatly for it.

When we think of forgiveness, we think that we have to excuse the other person; to pardon them and let them walk away without being punished. That if we do this, they'll get off completely free and that's not something we want to see happen. We want them to be punished. We want them to be held accountable for what they have done to us. We want others to know that we were wronged. In our minds, forgiveness means that justice will never happen, and that's something we're not prepared to accept. The same can be said about forgiving ourselves. We make mistakes, everybody does, but too often we beat ourselves up, annoyed by what we did, and hold on to our anger and pain as a punishment. This stems from a belief that we're not good enough. If this is you, I want you to know that you *are* good enough and you need to forgive yourself. Your best life is waiting.

Forgiveness is not about letting somebody get away

with what they've done. It is not about letting somebody walk away unpunished for their crimes. It is not about saying that what they did doesn't matter. It's not about not wanting justice.

Holding on to all of that hurt, pain, anger and resentment does three things: it hurts you; it prevents you from living your true potential; and it does nothing to affect the other person. I have heard it said that unforgiveness is like drinking poison hoping that it will kill the other person. It doesn't; it only kills you – slowly.

Forgiveness is simply the act of letting that emotion go. It doesn't change the reality of what happened. It just says that you choose not to be affected by it, that you will not be held a prisoner by an event from long ago.

Forgiveness can be painful. Sometimes we wrestle with that emotion, trying to let it go but at the same time hanging on to it. Sometimes emotions are buried so deep within us that it's a painful and exhausting journey to bring them to the surface and let them go.

Forgiveness can also be quick. Look at children in the playground. Someone hurts them and there are tears, but a minute later they're the best of friends again. They choose to let the emotion go. Often when we choose to let the emotion go, the memories surrounding the person or event fade away. We no longer think about them or what they've done and move on with our lives.

Forgiveness is freeing. When we chose to forgive, all we're doing is letting go of the negative emotions that we've held on to. When we let go of those emotions, we immediately feel lighter. Our stress and anxiety levels go down and we sleep better. We feel better about ourselves and life in general. Our health improves. Depression diminishes. Our energy levels go up and we get unstuck. Often problems we've been wrestling with either get resolved or simply go away. We experience breakthroughs – things we've been trying to make happen suddenly happen. Sickness disappears. We attract love into our life. People treat us better.

So how do we actually forgive? Is there a process that allows us to experience all of these benefits? Yes and no.

How to Let Go

For some, letting go can be just a case of mental assent – making a decision to let that emotion go. I have experienced this many times. I sit quietly and allow myself to fully feel that emotion. I then simply choose to let it go.

Often as I focus on experiencing any particular emotion, I feel a tension somewhere in my body. I have experienced that tension in my neck, arms, legs and feet, but mostly I experience it in my stomach, around my solar plexus. I then place all of my attention and focus on that feeling in my body and it quickly diminishes. As it does, I always feel lighter. I then keep repeating this until the emotion I have been feeling disappears. Sometimes I score the emotion from 1 to 10 and, with each round, I see the score getting lower until it's gone.

Often, though, I need to go deeper. When I know that I am holding on to negative emotion, pain and resentment due to someone else I find that I need to write them a letter. I never send those letters and they don't need to be sent. They need to be written, read out loud and then destroyed.

Growing up, I was deeply affected by the words of my mother. She struggled with her mental health and self-image and would project much of her angst on to me and my sister. She was never physically abusive to us and took care of all of our physical and financial needs. She was brilliant in that respect. At times when we got into trouble, she would defend us and take care of us, providing much-needed love and comfort. The problem was the emotional and spiritual abuse: telling us that we weren't good enough, that nothing we ever did was acceptable to her; constantly telling us that we weren't as good or as capable or as clever as our friends. I remember her saying once that she was going to leave all of her money to the dogs' home because we didn't deserve it.

I also experienced racism, often violent racism, on nearly a daily basis for 18 years. All of those negative words cut very deeply. Whoever said that 'Sticks and stones may break your bones, but words can never hurt you' was a fool. Words *do* hurt and, as a result of the bullying I experienced, I always felt I needed my mother's comfort and approval.

In later years she became a grandmother to my children and those of my siblings. In our eyes she was the world's best grandmother. Then one day she got sick, very sick, and a few weeks later she died.

I held her hand as she passed and, at that exact moment, my world imploded. I was angry and terrified all at the same time. The grief was overwhelming. Night after night I would find myself crying uncontrollably. This went on for eight years. My career stalled and my relationships suffered. I was angry all of the time. I didn't realise at the time that I still needed my mother's approval and that, without her being there, I couldn't get it.

One day I was receiving life coaching and my coach suggested that all of my life and career angst was probably connected to my mother. He was right and I knew that. He asked me to forgive her, but I couldn't and wouldn't.

Sensing my turmoil, he encouraged me to write a letter to her, read it out loud and then destroy it.

In that long letter I poured my heart out. Pages and pages were filled with anger, hurt and resentment. I held nothing back. All of the vitriol came pouring out. I was crying and, at times, could hear weird wailing sounds coming from deep within me. A lot of trapped emotion was being let go. Suddenly the anger stopped, and my words become more neutral, telling her about my kids and eventually becoming very positive, saying how much I loved and missed her. It took me over an hour but, by the end, all of my anger, pain and resentment had gone. I felt lighter and happier. The anger, hurt and resentment have never come back.

Over the next weeks and months, the change in me was obvious to everyone around me. I wasn't angry anymore. I had far more patience. I was more self-accepting. Stressful situations at work suddenly lessened and my career began to improve. I felt happier than I had done in years and the grief lifted. Years later that peace and joy has just kept increasing. I feel happier than ever before. Now when I think of my mother, I am filled with a love for her that staggers me.

What do you need to let go of? What emotions are trapped deep within you that are controlling you and preventing you from enjoying the life that you know you want and is available to you? Who do you need to forgive – yourself or others? Write a letter, read it out loud and then destroy it. Declare 'I choose to let these emotions go.'

Action points

- Each night write down everything you are worried about and give it over to God.
- Spend five minutes taking deep breaths.
- Forgive yourself for your mistakes.
- Practise letting go.
- Write more letters.

Having got out of our heads and let go of the past we are now free to deeply connect with our heart and decide what it is that we want from life, our purpose and what matters most.

CHAPTER 9

Step 5: Find Your Why

Living on purpose is living intentionally; deciding what you want out of life and then pouring all of your time, talent and energy into making that happen.

It's about waking up each day knowing where you want to go, what you have to do to get there, having the confidence to act and knowing why that's important to you. It's about being true to who you are on your best day and being that person every day. It's about having a vision for your whole life. It's about defining what success and happiness look like to you for everything that you regularly engage in and experience. It's about starting with the end in mind.

When we live intentionally our lives are filled with meaning and purpose, which leads to greater feelings of peace, joy and contentment.

Living intentionally requires that we connect with others in order to draw on the talent and passion of those around us to help us achieve our dreams. That requires that we develop a positive mental attitude and a pleasing personality that others want to help and be around. We can't do it on our own.

Living intentionally is about finding and following our 'why' – the reason behind everything that we do which gives our lives meaning and that requires us to focus our time on what is most important and learn to let go of what isn't. We learn to live by principles that enable us to be true to our values and develop habits that support those principles. We are then able to set goals that are most meaningful to us and can pursue them with full abandon. The exercises in this chapter will show you how to find your why.

Destinations, maps and compasses

In order to live intentionally we need a destination, a map and a compass. Our destination is where we want to go – our purpose. Our map shows us how to get there from where we are and our compass points us in the right direction.

Having all three is essential to making effective decisions. They allow us to choose from the multiple competing and deafening choices that are constantly before us. They allow us to effortlessly say yes to some things and no to others. They allow us to better manage our time, making the most of each day, month and year.

Knowing what we want and what matters most is of paramount importance to and always increases our quality of life and happiness.

The unexamined life

Most of us are living rudderless as we go through life. We are repeatedly blown from one course of action and direction to another, governed by our feelings. We are told that the grass is always greener by the external voices that tell us what we should want and desire. Our friends tell us that this is the way to go; the Internet tells us something different.

The unexamined life is possibly the greatest cause of unhappiness that I know of. Never to have taken the time to decide what's most important to you and why is a tragedy and the first step on a path to a life of regret and emptiness.

The greatest regrets of the dying are not the things that they did, but the things that they didn't do. They recognise that they poured their time, talent and energy into what they hoped would make them happy, only to find out that it didn't give them what they truly wanted.

I imagine that spending your life pursuing things that you thought would make you happy, only to find out that they didn't, must be very painful. Living with intention prevents this from happening.

We get to choose the game we play and then determine the rules by which that game is played. We get to live life in such a way that there are no regrets.

Choices

Not knowing where we're going – not having a why – without a map or compass, will always result in struggling to make decisions. If we don't know where we want to go, we'll always struggle to know what to say yes to and what to say no to.

Without that map we will always react to life instead of living intentionally and proactively. I'm not talking about seizing life's unexpected and wonderful opportunities, but rather going through life hoping that something good will happen to us instead of determining what good looks like and then going out to find it.

As a result of not living intentionally we find that our lives are without meaning. Not completely, of course, but in those quiet moments when we pause and reflect, we find ourselves wanting more; more joy, more peace, more meaning and more purpose.

We inevitably find that we need less to make us happy and contented but struggle to step off the path we're following, believing that we've travelled so far that it's not possible to find a way back. No matter how far off course you believe yourself to be, I want you to know that it's not too late – you're not too old and you are closer than you think to living a life of meaning and purpose. You are only ever one intention away.

Rediscovering our values and learning to live from them is the key to living a life of meaning and purpose.

Values

Author Hyrum W Smith says our values are 'what matters most' – they are our deepest held beliefs about what each of us determines to be of the greatest importance to us.

When we know what's important to us and build our lives around it, we are able to find and experience the deepest levels of meaning and purpose. We will know in our hearts that our time on earth has meaning and that what we do is of value to ourselves and others. We want to feel connected to something bigger than ourselves and living our values allows us to do that.

Our values allow us to differentiate what's important from what is really valuable. Your performance at work might be important to you, but your health or spending time with your family might be really valuable. Whatever you value, you pour your time, talent and energy into.

Our values determine what we stand for, what we'll fight for and what we'll ultimately defend.

Living true to our values is a cornerstone to high self-esteem. When we are true to ourselves, we are always able to look in the mirror and be content with what we see. No matter what others are saying and the pressure that they seek to bring on us, we are able to hold our head up high.

The advantages of knowing your values

Identifying our values gives us the chance to be able to reassess and prioritise our lives. We are able to identify where we are unhappy, off course and unfulfilled, and from this place we can begin to recreate the life we want.

We are able to see where our performance is out of line with our values, especially those areas where we are giving others permission to dictate what is of importance to us. We are able to see where we are functioning below our potential.

We are able to identify where we have actually been self-sabotaging. We can give ourselves permission to be happy and fulfilled and to follow our dreams. We are able to eliminate things that we previously thought very important to us and reorder our lives, focusing much more on what matters most.

Honouring our values leads to a life of peace, fulfilment, joy and happiness. If we dare ignore them or try to live in opposition to them, we will find ourselves increasingly stressed, worried and anxious, often leading to ill health.

Clarifying our values and living true to them offers us three great advantages over the unexamined life. It gives us our own personal North Star, a solid foundation and allows us to recalibrate.

Sailors are always able to get to where they want to go as long as they can see the North Star. They are able to chart a course based on this fixed point in the universe. Having your own North Star allows you to chart a course in life from where you are to where you want to be, no matter how difficult life gets or how big the storms that rage around you. You can look up and remind yourself of what's most important, see where you need to go and chart a course to get there.

Knowing your values is of limited worth if you don't live them intentionally. Building your life on what is most important and purposeful to you allows you to create a solid foundation that can never be shaken, even in the most difficult of times. Knowing what matters most provides us with a platform on which we can then build every aspect of our lives.

The Bible says, 'The wise man built his house upon the rock.' We need to stop and ask ourselves: are we building on solid rock or shifting sand?

Our values allow us to recalibrate at any time. It's easy

to get off course. We only need to be a couple of degrees off target and in time we'll find ourselves hundreds of miles away from where we want to be. In those times, knowing our values allows us to recalibrate.

We can look to our North Star, recognise that we're adrift and set a new course bringing us back to where we need to be.

Uncovering Your Core Values

As we discussed in Chapter 4, there are three levels of values: universal, adopted and core values (see page 61). Our core values are those that shape how think, behave and communicate. We know that everything we have in our lives is from the sum of all of our actions and that our actions are always determined by our beliefs. Living from our core values allows us to consciously create more of what we truly want in life and act in accordance with those desires.

There are many ways to uncover our core values. We can take online tests and work with a coach, but I've found that, with the hundreds of people I've worked with, using the following simple three-step method allows them to finally figure out their core values and create a road map to living them.

Step 1: Make a list

Write down everything that is meaningful and important to you. In doing so please don't try to judge your answers – you can do that later. For now, the goal is quantity not quality. Just write down everything that comes to mind.

- What is important to me?
- What do I like?
- What am I constantly drawn towards?
- What makes me angry and what's the opposite?
- What would those closest to me say is most important to me?

Group your list into clusters of words that sound similar or have similar meanings – clusters can also be just one word. Then choose the one word that best describes that cluster i.e. truth, honesty and integrity are similar sounding words that might mean the same thing to you. If so, choose one word that best describes that cluster. Writing your values on Post-it notes and sticking them on a wall can be really helpful.

Step 2: Explore your why

Once you have your list of values, it's time to uncover

those that are core to you. We do that by asking ourselves two questions:

1. What does this value mean to me?
2. Why is this important to me?

This may take some time, so please don't rush it. Enjoy the journey; I promise you that it will be totally worth the effort.

Step 3: Prioritise

From your list of values, pick out your top five and prioritise them. If you're struggling to prioritise them, you might find these two additional questions will be of help to you:

1. What is it like for you when this value is missing from your life?
2. What happens when people mistreat your value?

You might also like to use the values prioritisation table below. Write your top five values in the table and ask yourself 'Which is more important: value 1 or value 2, value 2 or value 1?' and continue doing this for all of your values.

Circle each answer and, when you're done, count them

up and it will help you to put them in order of importance. A fuller table and more exercises can be found in the accompanying workbook, which you can download for free at www.routesuk.com

1			1	2	1	3	1	4	1	5
2			2	3	2	4	2	5		
3			3	4	3	5				
4			4	5						
5										

Creating a Purpose Statement: Naming Your Why

Once you've uncovered your core values, I'd encourage you to live with them for a while and adjust the language as appropriate, for example changing the word 'honesty' to 'integrity' because it feels better. When you're happy, at least for now, that you know and understand your core values it's then really useful to create a purpose statement which will become your North Star and solid foundation – your why.

This is how I did this with my values, which over time I came to understand are spirit, adventure, belonging and service:

Spirit means to seek the presence of God, hear his voice and to respond unreservedly.

Adventure means to travel, set huge intentions and to live without regrets.

Belonging means to be part of a community of people that see, hear and accept me for who I am.

Service means to use my gifts and talents to help others fulfil their purpose and potential.

I have then brought all of that together in one statement which is to:

Live big, by faith, with friends in the service of others.

This is the purpose I have chosen for my life. It's my North Star – my why – and allows me to live on purpose. It's the gatekeeper by which I make all decisions and how I spend my time. Having a purpose statement is without doubt a complete game changer.

I would encourage you to put this book down and have

a go at creating your own purpose statement if you haven't already done so. Once you have done this, please take a moment to think about all the times in your life when you felt you were at your best. I'm confident that you will see that those were times when you were living true to your values. Creating and living true to your purpose statement is perhaps the key to living on purpose.

Action points

- Complete the values exercise.
- Write your purpose statement.
- Set new intentions.
- What new habits do you need to create?

CHAPTER 10

Step 6: Discover Your Gift

You have a gift, and when you align with your gift you move from routine boredom to a state of profound joy and happiness. Every day you wake up full of expectation, excited about what the day will bring, knowing that what you do matters and that you're owning your rightful place on this planet and making a difference.

We are standing at a global tipping point – where the power of technology and the Internet are enabling ordinary people to leverage their uniqueness, package their gifts and bring them to the world.

Your gift highlights the work that you're meant to do. It answers the 'What?' question. Once we know and own our gift, we can then align it with our purpose and mission to answer both 'Why?' and 'Where?'

Our innate gifts and talents need to be nurtured and developed throughout our life. When we see gifts in our children at an early age, we need to welcome, nurture and encourage them. Gifts of leadership and communication, nurture and compassion, design and creativity, emotional intelligence, practicality, and more, all need as much encouragement as we can possibly give. We need to provide opportunities for our children to engage with what they are fascinated with in order to help release both their gifts and their spirit.

For years, my daughter and I would sit outside a local coffee shop on a Saturday morning people-watching, asking each other who we thought they were, what they did, whether they were happy or not and trying to guess their names. Years later my daughter is still the most intuitive person I know.

Our gifts shape how we think and act

If you are gifted to work with people, you will want to spend time with people. You will always prefer meeting people face-to-face rather than over the phone, via Skype or through instant messaging. You will take time to be with people. You won't write that report if you can have a coffee and a chat with someone instead.

If you are gifted to work with information, you will always look for data before making a decision and to demonstrate what you are saying.

If you are gifted to work with your hands, you will often learn best hands-on.

All gifts are needed and of equal value

Sadly, society places greater value on scientific and academic abilities over artistic, creative and vocational abilities. Business also places greater value on these same gifts and less on the others. We call leadership, emotional intelligence and creativity 'soft skills'. Thankfully, this is beginning to change. The most sought-after skills of the future, if not now, will be problem-solving, innovation, creativity, communication and entrepreneurial leadership. There is nothing soft about those.

I remember every year going to my eldest daughter's parent–teacher evening and each teacher, except one, would tell me that she talked too much and needed to learn to be quiet. Each year, much to my daughter's embarrassment, I would ask the teachers, 'Thank you for noticing her gift as a communicator. We see that too. What are you doing to develop it?'

The teachers would look at me with completely blank faces, screw their eyes up and say something like, 'What? I don't know. She just needs to talk less.'

But one teacher was different. She was young, enthusiastic and had an ability to deeply understand the emerging gifts in her students. Nothing she saw was seen as negative. She only saw potential and did her best to draw that out, making each student feel that they mattered.

Imagine if Martin Luther King Jr had been told to sit down and shut up or Michelangelo to stop doodling or Martina Navratilova to sit still or Mother Teresa to stop dreaming.

We laugh, but it's happening every day. Maybe it happened to you. If it did, then I'm really sorry you went through that. Please be assured that it's never too late to step into your greatness and shine and be who you were created to be. When we step into the fullness of our gifting, we experience the favour of God on us and, as author and speaker Bishop T D Jakes says, 'One moment of favour is worth 10 years of labour.' You are never too old and it's never too late for you to do the work that you're meant to do.

Don't improve your weaknesses

Year after year this same story is being repeated, not only in classrooms but also in the workplace.

In many of our annual appraisals we're set goals that aren't in alignment with our top talents and, in addition, are asked to work on our weaknesses. There is little value in working on anything for which we have limited natural ability. It's a fool's errand. A friend of mine who worked with diamonds in London's Hatton Garden, would often crassly say, 'You can't polish a turd.' Rude, but correct.

Elephants can't climb trees, penguins don't run fast and squirrels make for bad swimmers. We wouldn't expect them to do what they're not naturally equipped to do. And yet we treat people differently; people are expected to be able to do everything and are judged poorly if they can't.

When we unduly focus on strengthening our weaknesses, we are trying to be someone that we were never created to be. We need to let others be brilliant at those things that are difficult for us to do, and allow them to shine brightly, and work together.

The Seven Motivational Gifts

There are seven unique motivational gifts and, when these gifts are used in combination with our values, they release our superpower.

The seven gifts are:

1. Intuition
2. Encouragement
3. Knowledge and Wisdom
4. Supervision
5. Creativity
6. Dexterity
7. Compassion

Each of us has a level of ability in each gift. That's why we can do anything that we set our minds towards. Being able to do something occasionally, does not mean, however, that we should build our life's work around it. The work that we love and are meant to do is found in aligning with our gifts and callings.

Gift clusters

Motivational gifts never work in isolation – they work in partnership with other gifts. We tend to have higher abilities in one to four gifts. When each gift cluster is then combined with the different elements of our personality, passions and callings, we see that every person is unique.

In my years of supporting people to discover their gift I have found that approximately 50 per cent of them have one strong gift; 35 per cent have two strong gifts; 10 per cent have three strong gifts; and some 5 per cent have four strong gifts. I believe that having one or two strong gifts is when the gift flows through you to others, but having three or four strong motivational gifts is indicative of what I call a 'true calling' – when *you* are the gift. I believe that we are seeing an ever-growing number of multi-gifted people who are beginning to awaken to their calling and infinite possibilities.

As an example of a gift cluster, if you have the gifts of intuition, knowledge and wisdom, and encouragement, you will tend to lead with your dominant gift.

In this case, it might be that the gift of intuition will perceive what's really happening in the lives of people and situations, connect the dots and make an intuitive decision about what needs to happen.

The gift of knowledge and wisdom will then find and suggest a solution. It will bring together everything you have ever learnt about the particular topic and will advocate the most appropriate course of action.

The gift of encouragement is then able to communicate the solution in such a way that the person will feel inspired to take action. The gift of intuition will also allow for dramatic and memorable communication.

The gift of knowledge and wisdom will break the information down into bite-sized chunks and help to prioritise them so that the person can see what to do next.

For a fuller description of each gift and a motivational gift assessment, please use the accompanying workbook which can be downloaded for free at: www.routesuk.com

Intuition

The motivational gift of intuition is the ability to solve

problems through the use of perception and intuition. It's the ability to see, hear and feel that which isn't obvious to others. It is the ability to 'connect the dots' from what's being intuited, to work out what's going on and, especially, what's going wrong. This gift is uniquely equipped to solve spiritual problems, especially the need for meaning, purpose and connection.

Your gift is being able to see straight to the heart of the matter and know exactly what the problem is. Your ability helps others to know what's really going on by being able to walk into any situation and quickly surmise the problems, character and nature of the systems, structures and people.

▶ *Your strengths*

- Ability to connect seemingly unrelated pieces of information to identify the problem.
- Unique ability to be able to see the consequences of a particular course of action.
- Can very quickly identify the heart of the matter.
- Ability to make people 'face up' to their problems and challenges.
- Persuasive and dramatic communicator.
- Can work alone for long periods of time.

- Will always try to do the 'right thing'.
- Pursues honesty, justice and the well-being of those under your responsibility.
- Acts on principles, won't compromise.
- High personal integrity.

Encouragement

The motivational gift of encouragement is the ability to inspire others through the use of creative communication and ideas. It's the ability to help others to see things from a different perspective. It is the ability to think on your feet, come up with lots of ideas and to communicate creatively. This gift is uniquely equipped to solve psychological problems, particularly the need for positive identity, self-image and esteem.

If you have the gift of encouragement you have been gifted to work with people, particularly those focused on wanting a better future. You always see the possibilities in other people, products and systems. You are able to take someone that is raw and undeveloped and, through your mentoring and coaching, make them highly effective. People are drawn to you because of how you make them feel. You bring out the best in them. You encourage, inspire and motivate others.

▶ *Your strengths*

- Ability to encourage others.
- Motivates others to achieve more.
- Inspirational and positive, a real 'can-do' attitude.
- Fluent and able communicator.
- Comes up with lots of creative ideas.
- Competent decision maker.
- Ability to work with individuals and groups.
- Accepting of people.
- Ability to see people's potential.
- Sets high standards.

Knowledge and wisdom

The motivational gift of knowledge and wisdom is the ability to apply knowledge to solve problems. It's the ability, through learning and research, to bring together different thoughts and share them in new ways that make it possible for others to learn and grow. You have the knowledge that others need to solve their problems. Your gift is wisdom – knowing exactly what to do.

You are fascinated by all that you see. You are motivated to learn and understand the world around you. You are drawn to many different sources of knowledge and a few topics in particular. You are able to bring together many strands of thinking and represent them in an evolved manner. You communicate well. Your knowledge builds a storehouse of wisdom that enables you to provide solutions to often complex problems. People seek you out for what you know.

▶ *Your strengths*
- Ability to study, research and analyse.
- Refining of ideas, systems and products.
- Ability to work in a structured, logical, systematic and accurate manner.
- Developing programmes.
- Self-disciplined and controlled.
- Ability to think critically.
- Can work in a clear and objective way.
- Able to detach yourself from the outcome.
- Can mine and validate truth, principles and wisdom from multiple sources.
- Sharp intellect.

Supervision

The motivational gift of supervision is the ability to manage people, projects and information. It's the ability to take vision and make it happen. You have the ability to create and implement strategies that turn vision into reality. You provide the 'how' – the details to make things happen.

You are equipped to handle responsibility, are task-focused and are not easily distracted from the task at hand and will get it done accurately, on time and within scope. You will assume responsibility where none exists. You know when to pivot and when to keep going.

▶ *Your strengths*

- Highly motivated and focused.
- Ability to plan, organise and bring structure to people and projects.
- Able to delegate and supervise.
- Clear communicator.
- Ability to handle simultaneous tasks.
- Natural leader.
- Long-range thinking.
- Accepts responsibility for work.
- Natural instinct when to keep going and when it's time to move on.
- Able to allow colleagues to receive praise.

Creativity

The motivational gift of creativity is the ability to bring together people, ideas and resources and create something greater than the sum of the component parts. It's an entrepreneurial ability to find and implement solutions to problems. This gift is uniquely equipped to work well to create art, aesthetic environments and wealth.

Enlightened givers naturally understand that they can make a huge difference through leveraging their time, talents and resources and the talents of others, and can build powerful communities and networks. You are equipped to bring something new to the world – an idea, product, service or experience.

This gift, while eminently practical, is also highly spiritual with the ability to create powerful positive intentions that help solve problems for other people, communities and organisations. This ability is strongest when the gifts of intuition, creativity and compassion appear in the same cluster.

▶ *Your strengths*

- Meeting the physical, emotional and spiritual needs of others.
- Ability to make money.

- Ability to give wisdom and guidance to those in your circles.
- Instinctively knows when an opportunity is right.
- Tremendous source of support and encouragement.
- Great steward of resources.
- Excellent sales and business abilities.
- Industrious, hard-working but also smart-working.
- Streetwise.
- Enjoys giving.

Dexterity

The motivational gift of dexterity is the ability to solve practical problems. It's the ability to know what needs to be done with a willingness to get on with it. It is the ability to implement practical solutions for complex problems. This gift is uniquely equipped to provide hands-on support.

This gift has a preference for working with the body, especially using the hands with objects. You demonstrate tremendous manual dexterity. You can always be relied on to get the job done. In bodily terms you are the hands of the body, lifting, moving, fixing, building, feeding and working. If you are not naturally drawn to working with your hands, you will prefer to be practical with a hands-on approach to most things.

You are naturally drawn to those who need practical assistance and projects that require practical things to get done. You may also have an ability to impart healing, comfort and restoration through your hands to others. You are naturally hospitable and that ability helps to create transformational environments.

▶ *Your strengths*

- Getting things done.
- Ability to see what needs to be done and a willingness to do it.
- Manual dexterity.
- Excellent memory.
- Works best on short-range projects.
- Hospitable.
- Highly energetic.
- Ability to support other people's vision through practical help.
- Will see whatever you are working on through to completion.
- Unique ability to impart healing, comfort and restoration through the laying on of hands.

Compassion

The motivational gift of compassion is the ability to solve emotional problems. It's the ability to be fully empathetically present with people during times of difficulty and distress to heal, comfort, build up and restore. This gift is uniquely equipped to work well with emotional problems, especially the need for renewed hope.

This gift is the ability to work with people, and to minister to their emotional, physical and spiritual needs. You have a highly developed sense of how groups and individuals are doing. You may not always know why something is wrong, but you always know when things are not right.

This gift is occasionally partnered with the gift of encouragement due to the different types of people that each gift is drawn to. Where it is, it denotes a real calling to work with people and should be taken seriously.

In bodily terms you are the heart. You provide love and connection. You are highly spiritual. People are drawn to you for love and comfort. You are very open (your openness and willingness to carry other people's burdens can lead to emotional burnout if not monitored).

You are motivated to see people restored to all that they can be. You are quick to champion and defend a cause.

You have a naturally cheerful nature and will often communicate through touch.

▶ *Your strengths*

- Huge capacity to provide love, comfort and encouragement to others.
- Can instinctively identify hurting people.
- Tremendous ability to work one-on-one with people.
- Can spot wrong motives in others.
- Will persevere when others give up.
- Trustworthy.
- Always looking for the good in others.
- Will do what it takes to assist others.
- Careful with words and encourages others to be the same.
- Kind and considerate.

Action points

- Make a list of the tasks you look forward to, enjoy and that energise you.
- Download and complete the motivational gifts questionnaire.
- Where can you bring more of these gifts to what you do?

- What was said about you that incorrectly labelled you? Reject it!
- Watch an online course to develop a new skill you're interested in.

Having discovered our gifts we need to align with the callings we have in order to do the work we're meant to do and make our special contribution. Happiness not only comes from doing work that is fully aligned with our gifts and talents but also in serving others. All ancient wisdom points to this truth – that when we serve others, we are actually serving ourselves. What we sow, we reap; what we do for others, will be done for us. When we help others, we will be happier and attract greater abundance into our lives.

In the next chapter we'll see how we release our superpower when we align our gifts with our values in the area of our calling.

CHAPTER 11

Step 7: Find Your Flow

All of life's greatest leaders used their gifts to serve others: Jesus, Gandhi, Mother Teresa, Rosa Parks, to name but a few, all found their purpose in life through giving their lives in the service of others.

Jimmy Carter, former President of the USA, said that he was happiest on his annual work project, and in particular when working as a volunteer with Habitat for Humanity. Over a 35-year period he and his wife worked alongside over 103,000 volunteers in 14 countries to build, renovate and repair 4,331 homes. You would think that being the most powerful man in the world and getting to enjoy the life that comes with that would be enough. Apparently, as good as it was, nothing beat working outdoors, climbing ladders, swinging a hammer and building homes for others.

Serving others opens a door to happiness, joy and a life of purpose, and that joy is best experienced through aligning our talents with service to the people and problems that matter most to us.

Sophie, a speaker and coach, had been repeatedly saying that she no longer enjoyed her work. She had days that seemed to spark joy, but increasingly she was feeling drained and uncreative. She was considering a career change but didn't know what else to do.

In discussion she talked about what she had done to recover from her divorce which had made her a much stronger person. She commented on the fact that so many people were going through messy divorces and they would benefit from her knowledge and experience. In that moment her eyes lit up as she realised that she still loved coaching and speaking, but the people she had been working with and the problems she was solving were no longer right for her. They failed to spark joy. She shifted her focus from entrepreneurs to women going through or recovering from divorce and she hasn't looked back.

Helping others involves people, problems and service. Intentionally helping others involves working with the people, problems and service that inspire and matter most to us.

Everybody needs help with something
Every person I have ever met has at least one heartfelt issue

that they are unable to solve. I have had the privilege to eat with street sleepers, millionaires and even a billionaire, all of whom spoke of a pain that wouldn't go away.

People everywhere live in quiet desperation, wanting help but not knowing where to turn or whom to ask. Their issues, problems and challenges are as deep and infinite as the entire human condition. Everybody needs help with something.

Their seeming inability to solve their problems often brings with it a sense of shame and failure, especially if others believe that they should be doing better. That shame often becomes debilitating. Something needs to change.

What do you wish were different about your own life but don't know how to make happen? Is it your health or finances, career or relationships? Have you tried to do something about it but failed? Are you hoping that something will click into place one day or maybe you've given up hope? Are you held back by fear?

How you can uniquely help others

Somebody somewhere, right now, is desperate for help and you have what they need. Everything you have gone through in life – each experience – has taught you something that could be of use to others. Every painful lesson you have learnt might be exactly what somebody needs to hear. That wisdom and experience have given you a message that the world wants to know.

Have you held the hand of a dying relative? Have you experienced a difficult childbirth? Have you lost weight, changed career, survived multiple redundancies, started a business, made or lost a fortune, found your soulmate, gone through relational difficulty, passed exams, experienced disease? Everything you have been through in life is an object lesson that can help others. What have you been through that has changed you and made you stronger? What would you like to share with others?

Passion is the desire to invest our time, talent and energy in what matters most. Every passion is like an internal compass, pointing to the people and problems that we are shaped to solve. Our gifts and talents, at the same time, act like magnets attracting to us the people that need our help. Who regularly seeks your help? What problems do people keep bringing to you? Which people and problems speak to you and call to you? Dare to follow your heart and see what happens. Who knows, maybe you were born for such a time as this.

My friend Daniel experienced depression as a teenager. He tried to take his life, thankfully he failed. Years later he felt inspired to write a blog post about his experience which was read by hundreds of people. His employer was so impressed that they gave him time to write and speak more about it. That has led to him becoming a mental health ambassador, speaking widely at conferences and meet-up groups. His message is one of hope and possibilities, and people everywhere are looking to him for help and advice. He repeatedly says that he never sought this recognition; all that he ever wanted to do was just share his story. He intuitively felt that somebody needed to hear it.

Often the people we are here to serve are earlier versions of ourselves; people wanting the same things we do and experiencing the same internal challenges that we experienced. Those people, that earlier version of our self, need what we learnt when we found a way through.

Flow

When we're doing the work we're meant to do and serving the people that we're meant to serve for the reasons that matter most to us, we experience a state of flow, when everything seems effortless, time seems irrelevant and we don't get tired. We get more done and, regardless of how hard we work, we feel stronger and more energised afterwards.

When we're in flow we experience deep levels of joy, meaning and purpose. Our work satisfies us, it directly helps those we serve and indirectly creates and sends out ripples of profound benefit to people we'll never meet, never know about or have any idea we've helped.

Let me explain... The honey bee goes to work each day with four things on her mind:

1. Doing what she loves.
2. Following her passion.
3. Focusing on what matters most.
4. Achieving a goal.

Doing what she loves

The honey bee loves to fly; it's what she loves the most. Soaring high, floating on the breeze, twisting, turning, looping – she lives for it all. Each day, she chats with the other bees, recounting stories of hazardous flights, breathtaking manoeuvres, narrow misses and daring escapes from children and wasps. They inspire each other to go higher and further than they've been before. She loves what she does and is good at it. She doesn't spend her time or energy engaged in tasks and activities that she doesn't enjoy or is not good at.

Following her passion

She loves to fly, but it's flowers that fascinate her. She's been deeply interested in them since she can't remember when. She knows and instantly recognises hundreds of flowers by sight. She knows which smell great and which don't! She knows which ones easily yield the most nectar and which are a pain to work with. She knows at what time of day and in which part of the garden and changing season each flower blooms. She's been interested in other plants, even trees, but she always comes back to flowers. It gives her tremendous satisfaction to fly from one flower to another, all day long.

Focusing on what matters most

Our honey bee understands that she is one bee in a colony

of bees. Each one has a role to play in ensuring that they all survive and thrive. The queen bee, honey bees and the worker bees all do their bit. It is important to her to be of service to others.

It's also important for her to be seen, heard and valued by her community, to know that she belongs. She loves that others are always pleased to see her. Nothing beats returning to the hive at the end of the day and catching up with the gang.

Focusing on what matters most gives her a real sense of meaning – her 'why'. Knowing that no matter how small her individual part, she is making a direct contribution, she is part of a tribe and is significant in the big scheme.

Achieving a goal

She understands that she serves the colony and the major requirement of the colony is to get enough nectar to meet their needs. Without it they will cease living. Every day she sets herself a goal to collect as much nectar as she can. She's not competing with anyone else. It's an unbeatable feeling to have such a tremendous sense of purpose, to go out every day and bring back nectar to the hive, knowing that the nectar is being used to feed, heal and grow the colony. She plays a vital role. She's a bee on a mission.

Like the honey bee, when you focus your efforts around your talent, passion, values and service to others, you will experience a profound sense of deep satisfaction, meaning and purpose, and connection to others through your work. You'll find that you rise early with a great sense of anticipation and drift off each night into a deep and peaceful slumber.

When you find a role that allows you to play to your strengths, you'll discover that you'll create two levels of impact – direct and indirect – and also release your superpower.

Every day, when the honey bee brings home nectar to be used by the colony in order for them to survive and thrive, she creates direct impact. She serves a specific group, solves their most immediate and pressing problem and, in doing so, is creating massive direct impact. She's saving lives.

Whenever we get in motion, we create motion. It's the ripple effect. We throw a stone into a pond and there's immediate and direct impact – the splash. Then there's the secondary and indirect impact as the ripples spread out, one after another, moving slowly across the pond until they touch the bank. If you do it enough the pond becomes a stream and the stream eventually becomes a river and the river brings life wherever it goes.

The honey bee creates direct impact for the colony she serves, but I suspect that she has little or no idea of the sheer magnitude of the indirect impact she creates on a daily and global scale. When she flies from flower to flower and plant to plant collecting the nectar, she's also picking up pollen on her body and wings which she transfers to other plants, allowing pollination to take place and allowing the plants to reproduce and grow, which provides food for the earth and soaks up carbon dioxide and releases oxygen. Thanks in part to her efforts, life on earth continues. She's saving billions of lives.

Her superpower is 'sustaining life'. Likewise, when you get into motion and focus your efforts on serving other's you'll create both direct and widespread indirect impact. You'll make your own unique contribution and be doing the work that you're meant to do.

Uncovering Your Superpower

When we align our gifts, passion and values in the service of others we create the perfect environment to release our superpower. Everybody has one and it's the driving intention behind everything that you do. It's your genius and it's what you bring to everything that you do. It's the outcome you create when you're doing the work that you love and are meant to do.

Our superpower is the gift we bring to the world. There is an ancient story that says before God created the world He looked down from heaven and saw the entire history of the world unfold before Him. As He did, He saw people crying out to Him in prayer and desperation for help and in response He created you. You were His greatest creation – you are the answer to somebody's prayers. When He created you in your mothers' womb, He gave you the perfect gifts and talents that you would need to help those people. He then birthed you in the exact point in history and geography for you to be the change that the world needs. No one else can do exactly what you can do.

All superheroes have a weakness. Superman would lose his abilities when he was around kryptonite. Wonder Woman was rendered helpless when a man bound her bracelets together and the Human Torch struggled around asbestos.

What we are called to help others with, is the very thing we often struggle to do for ourselves. It's the dark side of our superpower and there is a reason for this. The world doesn't need another failed leader telling us what to do and doing the exact opposite when he thinks nobody's looking. The world needs much more than our passion. It needs people that can bring about effective transformation through what they do and say. Words are not enough.

The world needs people who are living examples of their own message – they walk the talk. They have paid the price and done what is necessary to get to where they are and to do what they purport to do. We want people who are anointed not self-appointed.

When we overcome the things that hold us back, we then have earned the right to talk about them. We can now bring a message of hope. When we overcome, we walk in greater moral and positional authority that backs up our message. When we reach this place, we are no longer offering broad concepts, talking about that which we know of but have failed to experience, but are able to bring about an impartation of grace through the words that we say. We can't give away what we don't have. When we have mastered our own dark side, we can then freely and magnificently help others to do the same.

There have been many times in our lives when we have been releasing our superpower through the work and activities that we've been involved in. Those times were those moments in life when we were fully engaged in what we love to do, fascinated with what we were engaged with, and it mattered to us.

In the accompanying workbook (which can be downloaded for free at www.routesuk.com) you will find an exercise that will greatly assist you in discovering your superpower. Below is a short version to help you to find and name your superpower in three simple stages.

Stage 1

Reflect back over your life and identity seven times when you were involved in a work, task or activity that you enjoyed doing and which mattered to you.

Write a short paragraph (or bullet points) describing the event, focusing specifically on what you were doing and why it was important. In doing this we allow our subconscious mind to connect the dots and help reveal to us our superpower.

You might find it helpful to trigger these memories by thinking through everywhere you have lived, worked and were educated.

▶ *Example*

When I was 14, I entered a public speaking competition. I spoke passionately about anti-vivisection. I researched my subject, wrote my speech and refined and practised every night for two weeks.

On the night of the competition I was first to speak. The lights were dimmed and a spotlight was put on me and I started to speak. It felt fantastic. I sensed that people were listening and hanging on to my every word. I tried to challenge and inspire the audience to change their views. After six other people had spoken the results were announced and I had won.

This was important to me because I felt I was making a difference, receiving respect and being on an adventure.

Stage 2

Choose the three statements below (or write your own) that best describe your superpower as identified in Stage 1. This is not a definitive list but a starting point.

Advancing ideas	Uncovering information	Investigating problems
Researching solutions	Creating meaning	Advancing knowledge
Fostering understanding	Pushing back boundaries	Uncovering truth
Seeing the big picture	Getting to the heart	Seeing possibilities
Removing barriers	Unlocking potential	Revealing greatness
Proclaiming freedom	Speaking life	Imparting love
Creating environments	Energising action	Creating joy
Facilitating understanding	Uncovering callings	Releasing spirit

Creating world changers	Opening up trust	Starting conversations
Awakening spirit	Facilitating change	Offering care
Giving love	Encouraging success	Healing wounds
Helping others	Inspiring success	Creating beauty
Initiating adventures	Restoring hope	Alleviating suffering
Shaping environments	Solving problems	Creating peace
Growing opportunities	Building structures	Investigating possibilities
Advancing ideas	Defending truth	Translating concepts
Birthing confidence	Creating meaning	Facilitating dreams
Analysing data	Developing connections	Building bridges
Inspiring warmth	Investigating alternatives	Engaging hearts
Designing lives	Digging deeper	Polishing diamonds

Stage 3

How you best describe your superpower is entirely up to you. It must, however, be of your own choosing.

Your chosen name or statement for your superpower may be literal or descriptive (metaphorical), but it should always contain one word that best describes the action you take and the other to describe what you are taking action on i.e. 'unlocking potential'.

You may have to also include words like 'the', 'to' or 'it', in order to connect your words i.e. 'Pushing back *the* boundaries', 'Getting *to the* heart.'

You might have to do some adjustments to get to the statement that best describes your superpower. From your selected descriptions score each one out of 10 (with 10 being the highest). Take the one with the highest score and write it down in the space below. Experience has shown me that once you score a 9 or higher, you've got it! If your score is 8 or lower, you might need to work on your statement a bit more. As you grow in your appreciation and understanding of your superpower, you might like to revisit it occasionally and see if you want to develop the language. For over 20 years I described my superpower as 'unlocking potential' and, as I've developed my understanding of it through experience, I have changed the language to 'releasing spirit', which feels more empowering.

My superpower is:

_____

_____

Action points

- Complete the superpowers exercise.
- What problems are you motivated to solve?
- Which people are you inspired to serve?
- What outcomes do you want to create?
- What can you do to start now, use what you have and do what you can?

We've looked at seven proven strategies to help you get unstuck, let go of fear, find your superpower and life's purpose. Now it's time for you to take the final step and bring them all together in an intentional purpose project designed by you in order to unlock your potential and live your purpose. It's time to get unstuck and move once more in the direction of your dreams.

CHAPTER 12

Take Action

Throughout 2018 I had increasingly felt that something had to change in my life, but I wasn't too sure what it was that needed to change or how to bring about that change. I'd been here before and knew that if I didn't do something quickly I would get stuck.

I still loved my work, but increasingly felt that it was becoming stale. It no longer brought the level of joy to my life that I'd previously experienced. I wasn't unhappy; I was restless and ready for something new.

I realised that I was at the turning point called 'significance' – I was successful and had helped many hundreds of people but there was a deep emptiness gnawing at me, making me feel that I hadn't achieved what I really wanted in life. I knew that there was a much deeper work that I was called to but the busyness of life, with its demands and responsibilities, was drowning out the clear message my intuition was trying to give to me.

From experience and the work that I do with others at crossroads, I knew what I had to do – to intentionally take time to slow down, re-energise, get out of my head and reconnect with what I love to do and with what matters most. So I created what I call a 'purpose project' in order to get unstuck and figure out what I needed to do next.

What are purpose projects?

Purpose projects are planned periods of time in which we intentionally bring more of what we love to do, and what matters most, back into our lives. These are times when we reconnect with what brings us joy and gives our life meaning.

When we do this, we naturally slow down, get out of our heads and back into our hearts and feel totally re-energised. Dynamic purpose projects also combine the two additional elements of contribution and personal growth that are most effective in helping us to find ourselves again.

How do they work?

Purpose projects last anywhere from a couple of days to a whole year. Most of mine have been about a week long, some have only lasted a few days over a long weekend and two have been as long as eight weeks. Generally, I've found that taking at least two weeks is most effective when needing to get unstuck, feel re-energised and gain the clarity and confidence needed to make big changes.

My purpose project centred on a 10-day trip to India during which I would spend time with my family, visit the orphanage we'd help to set up 20 years ago, meet some social entrepreneurs running amazing projects, reconnect with old friends, visit a new city, speak at a couple of conferences and accept an invitation to advise a network of pastors wanting to know what I felt God was saying to them.

After an amazing 10 days doing all of this and having a few wild mini adventures – driving a big red tractor on a farm, swapping skincare tips with a eunuch, eating crabs on the beach watching the sun go down, and much more – I came home knowing exactly what I needed to do next. I stepped away from my job, started writing this book and launched two new ventures.

Purpose projects are wide-ranging and unique to the individual: Russel went to Paris for a week to walk, talk and pray and came back so changed that he then dedicated his life to helping others as a mentor and speaker; Mary dedicated a few days to bring together her love of music and community and on returning started a travelling music group that brings help, hope and support to isolated communities; Sanjay invited a bunch of friends round to his house for a day to explore yoga, art and healthy food, which led to a change of career and launching an alternative lifestyle community; Steve set up his purpose project to include volunteering at a leadership development conference – his interactions with the speakers inspired him so much that he launched a Saturday morning sports coaching programme for disadvantaged young people; Sarah set aside three days to travel to different artistic cities in the UK, which inspired her to start her jewellery business.

It's possible to know all of the strategies required to change our lives, but until we take action nothing happens. Intentional purpose projects are one of the best things you can do to get clear and confident about what to do next.

There are three phases to a purpose project:

1. Planning: choosing the things we want to engage with in our project, communicating our intentions to others and asking for support.
2. Participation: enjoying the journey and detaching from the outcomes.
3. Active learning: re-envisioning our lives and taking action.

Planning

It's essential to prepare for your purpose project in advance. As they say, 'Failing to plan, is planning to fail.' I have found that this planning doesn't need to be overly complicated and can be fun, especially with the help of a trusted friend and a few G&Ts.

All transformative purpose projects involve using our gifts, talents and passions to serve others and live on purpose. Four dynamics – talent, values, contribution and a big hairy audacious goal – are always required for a successful outcome. (Remember the example of the honey bee on page 192.)

Purpose projects require time away (where possible) from our normal routine and a reprieve from our regular roles and responsibilities. They also need to be challenging – doing something that you haven't done before so that you face a few fears and, in overcoming them, you feel empowered and grow. Doing new things keeps us learning and feeling young. When was the last time you did something for the first time? The longer that was, the more challenging it is to try something new. Leaders are learners.

During my India trip I wanted to see family and friends – this would engage my value of belonging, being with people that see, hear and value me for who I am. I planned to speak at a couple of conferences and personally coach a few leaders – which would allow me to do what I love doing the most, speaking and mentoring. I chose to volunteer at our old orphanage and to meet with a social entrepreneur working for an Indian NGO – as part of the contribution element of the project as well as honouring my value of service. Being asked to speak to a group of pastors who wanted to know what God was saying to them would be the really scary part, knowing that there is always a risk of getting it wrong and the consequences if people make big decisions on what you've told them.

I chose to go abroad because I love to travel. All of which I felt would make for a truly great purpose project. In going to India I hoped that reconnecting with what matters most, what I loved to do, following my purpose and getting well and truly outside my comfort zone would help me to get unstuck, let go of any limiting beliefs and figure out what to do next.

Before I started the planning process, I talked with my wife about my intentions and asked her if she would be happy to support me, knowing that being away from home for two weeks would impact her and the family. Having her support always allows me to fully commit to my purpose projects and really enjoy them, as I support hers.

Once I had the idea, I booked my tickets, had my jabs and got on the plane.

Participation

Having planned your purpose project you then need to go and do it, as it's very easy to not fully commit and to scale back your intentions as you go through your project.

On my first night in India the hotel room was dark and unclean; there was no hot water, no toilet paper and too many mosquitos. Everything in me wanted to give up and go home. I was tired and hungry, and I felt lonely. My wife often tells me nothing looks as bad after a good night's sleep. She's right. The next morning I bought some toilet paper and mosquito repellent and accepted the fact that I would have to wash in cold water – it's amazing how quickly you can wash when you need to!

Throughout the trip I was regularly confronted with situations that put me significantly outside my comfort zone – speaking at meetings in people's homes where the poverty was staggering, getting soaked by torrential rain and having to deal with the heat and humidity. None of this was new to me – I have been to this rural area of India on multiple occasions – but I hadn't been on this type of trip for a long time and it was unusually stressful and demanding, forcing me to have to continually make the decision to commit, not give up and see where it took me.

Participation is about being fully present to what's happening to you and around you at all times. It's allowing yourself to feel all of the emotions that your project stirs up in you, both positive and negative. It's also about going at a sustainable pace which allows you the time to think and reflect. Don't rush to get it completed – this is not a task, it's a journey. Learning to enjoy the journey is transformative and can be highly cathartic. Remember to stop and breathe and fully experience everything.

A purpose project is also about saying yes to unexpected opportunities and seizing all that life has to offer.

I'll never forget the experience of driving a huge red tractor as fast as it would go across the organic farm we were visiting, while the farm worker who was sitting next to me screamed at the top of his voice, 'Sir, please slow down!' In that brief moment something unlocked in me. I was a child again. As I laughed and screamed at the top of my voice, I felt a sense of joy and freedom that I hadn't had for years. It was exhilarating, but not for him!

When you are engaged in a purpose project built around what you love to do and what matters most, you will experience tremendously positive emotions. You might also cry a lot. Each time you do, give yourself permission to experience every emotion deeply and fully. As you do, you release their power to do deep and transformational work. Every fully felt positive emotion restores your soul.

Reflection

It is very important to take the time to reflect throughout your purpose project, to identify what you are learning from it and what changes you might now need to make, if any. I always recommend reflection both during and after your project.

There is an inherent danger of overanalysing your experiences and trying to connect dots that aren't necessarily there. This comes from entering your project with preconceived notions about what needs to happen and the outcomes you want to create.

Reflective learning requires a letting go of any expectations, detaching from any desired outcomes and simply learning to be present in the journey and to how you feel at any given moment, in particular listening to your inner voice as it seeks to tell you of the mysteries of your heart and the unlived dreams and steps to take. It will always talk to you about the things that you most need to hear.

We long for this inner guidance and are often fearful of what it has to say. When we are fully engaged in what we love to do and with what matters most, our inner voice never scolds or chastises, but speaks like a child with pure joy, gently inviting us to go deeper and much further than we have ever been before in the pursuit of bliss. Your inner voice wants you to experience pure joy.

Throughout my purpose project in India I would regularly practise reflective learning by writing down my thoughts in my journal and taking lots of photos of all the places I went to and the people I met. Every morning I would take the time to sit quietly and think about the day ahead, the people I would meet, look to see if I was stressed or worried about anything and then, after being present to all of that emotion, I would simply let it all go. I would allow myself to experience every single emotion and would just try my best to let them go.

Some of those emotions were dark and powerful, fearing people and situations. My heart would race as I allowed myself to feel these emotions, then I let them go. Every time I let them go, I found that when they came back, if they did, they were less intense. Eventually some of them never came back and situations I thought would definitely happen never occurred.

At the end of each day I would look at all of the photos I had taken and think about what I had experienced, how it made me feel and what I had learnt about myself, the world and my place in it. I would jot down my thoughts, reactions and any questions it brought up as I went along. Over the next days I would hold those questions like an intention, knowing that as I did, the answers would come.

As I reflected each day, I realised that I kept asking myself the question, 'What next?', longing to know where to go and what to do, desperate to move on from the crossroads that had me stuck and not knowing what to do next.

As I kept holding that question as an intention, I was particularly drawn towards the interactions I'd had with two people I had met: a lady on the flight out and a widow who asked to speak with me. Both interactions triggered a deep primordial longing to do different work. Almost a feeling that this was the time to do the work that I was created to do, to work with people on a deeper transformational level and to change the message I was bringing to the world. I felt that I wanted to move away from mainly transactional coaching (helping people achieve goals – changing careers and starting businesses) to helping people let go of the lies that are holding them back and finally become who they really are. I was also stunned by the desire that kept growing in me to launch a spiritual community for those wanting more out of life and to journey together.

Everything in me wanted to dismiss those feelings as they felt like they belonged to an old dream I once had. It felt like I was going backwards, but as I allowed myself to feel them, I could sense my inner voice telling me that this was the direction in which I needed to go. Every time I felt this, I would write down my thoughts, give thanks for what I was hearing and ask for greater wisdom and guidance.

Returning home I gave myself a few days to recover and then began to engage with the deeper process of reflecting on what I had learnt about myself, what was missing from my life, what to let go of and what I needed to do differently.

I realised that the work that I was doing was good, but I knew that good is often the enemy of great and that the time had come to let it go. I knew that there was a new message that was beginning to surface and I needed time to hear and discover it. As a result, and with the backing of my wife and family, I stepped away from my work and gave myself a three-month sabbatical to transition to the next stage of my journey.

12 amazing and life-changing benefits of completing a life purpose project

1. Reduce stress and anxiety.
2. Eliminate depression.
3. Feel re-energised.
4. Forgive others.
5. Let go of the past.
6. Learn to live in the present.
7. Find your purpose.
8. Awaken dreams.
9. Change career.
10. Follow your passion.
11. Start something.
12. Tell fear to go to hell.

First Steps

For change to happen you need to take action. I would encourage you to start small and work up. That can best happen by making the decision to do something meaningful in the next two weeks. That gives you enough time to research and make a plan but not enough time to get disheartened and want to give up.

Setting aside half a day or a full day is just enough time

to experience many of the benefits that come from engaging with what you love to do and with what matters most.

Think of two or three things that you love to do (talent) and make a list of what fascinates you (passion) and what matters most (values). Then think of a cause that you are particularly interested in or a problem that you see in your world that you would like to help solve (contribution). Having done that, hold an idea party (wine, cake and raucous laughter) with a few friends to come up with 20+ ideas that would allow you to bring all of this together. Pick the one that is doable and slightly scary, enlist the help of a few people to keep you accountable and go out and do it.

Give a talk, run a workshop, volunteer, make something, sell something, maybe travel somewhere new. You are only limited by your imagination. It doesn't have to be anything particularly huge or expensive, just meaningful to you and big enough for you to feel a bit afraid. Many of my female clients talk about this as the moment when you have to put on your 'big knickers' and get it done. My male clients have absolutely no idea what this means!

I first met Judith at a workshop I was giving at the University of Cambridge about how to find the work you love and are meant to do. At the end I challenged the students to undertake a 30-day challenge (a forerunner to what I now call purpose projects) to use their time, talent and energy and set a goal to do something meaningful to help others.

Judith approached me afterwards and said that she had her final exams in a few weeks and so would need to complete her challenge after that. Only a few days later, she contacted me again saying that she couldn't wait and that she wanted to do something to help the homeless and had already started.

Over the next few weeks Judith engaged on a daily basis with her purpose project. She persuaded friends to sleep out on the streets as part of a national campaign to highlight homelessness. She befriended a number of rough sleepers, volunteered at a local night shelter, sold *The Big Issue*, helped to raise money for a homeless man to buy a guitar so he could sing at a local talent show, and much more. (You can hear her talk about her experience at www. routesuk.com/videos)

As a result of her purpose project she found clarity about her career choice – wanting to help the homeless – and gained the confidence to apply for a job that would allow her to do just that. She secured a job with a housing association and was able to talk about her experiences at the interview which clearly set her apart from all of the other candidates.

Congratulations for getting this far. Aligning your life with the seven proven strategies in this book will create profound change in your life, unlock your potential and allow you to life your purpose – but is there more?

There is one final decision to make: will you surrender to your calling?

CONCLUSION

I don't remember the exact date, but I'll never forget the day I found my calling.

Walking around a local market in China in 1991 I turned a corner, and my wife and I found ourselves looking at the one of the most sickening and depressing sights I've ever seen. In front of us was a little girl, maybe 18 months old, propped up against a wall, clothed in scant, dirty and pitiful rags. Her hair was long and dishevelled, knotted and matted. She was covered in mud and dust and her hair was crawling with insects. There was no light in her eyes, she didn't smile, maybe she never had, and there was fear written all over her face.

I stared at her, trying to take in the situation. It didn't take long to understand what was going on, as there was a begging bowl and a small sign propped up beside her, clearly asking for money. That was the least offensive part for, as I gazed at her, my eyes struggled to take in the enormity of what I was seeing. Her arms had been amputated at the elbows and one leg was severely disabled.

My heart broke. I didn't know what to do. I'd like to

think I put some money into her bowl, but I just can't remember. I'd hate to think I walked away, but I think in that moment I probably did, but I've never forgotten her and have thought about her regularly ever since.

Talking with our translator, she told us that this was not actually uncommon. Rural families in poverty simply didn't have the money to care for a disabled child. Looking after them was a burden on their meagre resources and putting them out to beg was their only solution.

Somebody needs to do something

We didn't have children at the time, but we still struggled to think how on earth this could be the best option as a parent. I was shocked and appalled but also challenged.

Riding on the train back to Hong Kong I said to my wife, 'Surely somebody must do something about this? There has to be people with the talent, passion and determination to do something about this.'

Over the next months I thought about little else. And in time various insights repeatedly came to me with profound clarity. Waking or sleeping I saw an army of ordinary superheroes using their time, talent and energy to solve the world's biggest and most pressing problems. I saw people with the passion to be entrepreneurs, starting businesses that would create jobs and lift whole communities out of economic poverty. I saw people with the passion to be politicians, working with governments to find solutions to these issues. I saw people with the talent and passion to be family and social workers, teaching people how to take care of their children.

I saw artists creating art that caused people to stop and think about what was going on and I saw writers writing books and articles that made people want to sit up and take notice. I saw film-makers and songwriters telling the world of the need for change, and I saw teachers and parents training young people how to stop and prevent injustices.

In every sphere of society I saw people using their talents and passion to do something to solve these problems. As they did, I am sure I saw the face of God smiling.

Saying yes to my calling

Heading home I couldn't stop thinking about what I had seen. The little girl was constantly there in my mind, and always before my eyes. Every night I would lie awake thinking, wondering, worrying about her. Decades later, she's still there. I would like to think that her life got better but I'm frightened that it didn't. More than anything I'd like to know her name.

I realised that I needed to do something about it, and I made the decision that I would devote my life to this, but I had no idea what to do or where to start.

Three months later I woke up early with a sentence running around in my head: 'Put people in roles where they can do the work that they're meant to do.' I knew what I had to do and what my first step would be – to train as a coach.

Little did I know the adventure that decision would take me on. I've been on that journey to make my calling a reality for nearly 28 years. It's taken me around the world. I've started businesses and charities to help people to find and do meaningful work. I've created workbooks and designed creative workshops and innovative programmes. I've given countless talks, trained hundreds of coaches and mentored thousands of people, and I hope that the journey will continue.

This Is Your Time and This Is Your Moment

I believe with all of my heart that you are here for a reason; that before the foundation of the world, God chose you and set you apart for a plan and a purpose. You are His answer to the prayers of a hurting world. You have been given gifts and talents, dreams and passions, all designed to point you in the direction of the people, problems and situations where you can make a significant impact. We may never fully solve these problems in our lifetime, but we'll do our very best to at least make a dent in them.

For too long, so many of us have been waiting for a sign or to hear a voice telling us this is the way, this is the path we are to take – but that sign has never come. We've been waiting for permission from others to shine and be brilliant – but that permission hasn't been given. We've looked to others to tell us what we can and can't do – and limited our glorious potential.

I am here today to tell you that your calling is yours and yours alone to make. You get to choose the purpose you want for your life. You get to choose which vehicle to pour all of your time, talent and energy into. There is no right or wrong path. There is no judgement or punishment waiting for you if you choose the 'wrong' path – indeed, there is no wrong path.

There is no one path

There are better paths, but no one path. Those better paths are those that bring you joy, that cause you to wake up each day full of peace and happiness. Choose purposes that take you down those paths. Choose purposes that allow you to do what you love and are meant to do. Work in fields that allow you to pursue your fascinations. Work to help people and solve problems that truly matter to you. Surround yourself with people who love and get you. Go where you're celebrated. Do everything with meaning. We only have one life and we need to live it well.

It's not too late

There is a song in you that is still waiting to be sung; a story waiting to be told. One of the greatest lies we've been told it that it's too late. It's not. You're never too old to begin to unfold your wings and fly. The best time to start was yesterday and, failing that, the next best time is now. All it takes is a single intention and decision to change your life forever. Are you ready to say yes to your best life and calling?

Saying yes to your calling

Those people that change the world in small but meaningful ways have all said yes to their calling and surrendered to it.

The army that I see is a force for good – a countless sea of ordinary superheroes who have said yes to their calling and are living to make it happen. Each one of them dared to look out at the world in front of them, saw the people and problems that inspired them, saw possible places where they could make a meaningful contribution and made the conscious decision to say yes.

Making a decision to follow your calling starts with saying yes. Then it means having to say no to other opportunities that might be good but ultimately are obstacles on the path to greatness. Making a decision always brings with it the fear of loss. We believe that if we say yes to one thing, it means we're saying no to others. That's not true. Everything is possible, but not at the same time. We're never saying no to other possibilities, we're just saying 'not now'. Saying yes means that we're giving ourselves permission to follow our dreams, to see where they take us and, if they don't take us where we thought they would, we can always change course. Never fear saying yes to your best life and calling.

Having said yes, we then need to stay committed and eventually surrender to the place where we accept that we were born to do this. Our being here at this time is part of a much bigger plan and we don't fight it. We no longer walk in fear. We know who we are and why we're here and we delight in it.

Three ordinary superheroes

Marina Pallares is the CEO of www.actingnow.co.uk, a social theatre company working to transform the lives of young people, those with considerable learning difficulties and those at risk of social exclusion. She works tirelessly to support others to live life to the full.

As a teenager growing up in Spain, she readily admits that she lost her way and found it hard to stay out of trouble. One day a teacher reached out to her and encouraged her to join a drama group, which she says changed her life forever. Through this small group she began to discover her talent for acting and was soon recognised for her incredible abilities. Leaving school she trained at a professional conservatoire but quickly realised that life on the professional stage wasn't for her.

Realising that her passion was to help others, in particular young people at risk of social exclusion, she began to search for opportunities that would allow her to do just that. Thinking that drama therapy might be right for her she moved to England to pursue her master's degree. On graduating, she looked for a social theatre company to join but couldn't find one and was faced with the decision to either start one herself or go and do something else.

I first met Marina when she was at the crossroads of

both direction and crisis – a very difficult combination to successfully transition. She told me of her dream but was very hesitant in stepping out not knowing many people and having limited resources.

Marina says that finding her calling wasn't so difficult – it presented itself to her in the form of young people who other people no longer believed in. Saying yes to her calling took courage, more than she thought she had, but she did it. It was more than saying yes, it took a decision to surrender to her calling, which meant saying no to other opportunities and daring to let go of the fear and insecurities and become the woman she was born to be.

Cansu Karabiyik is the Chief Executive of non-profit www.laugh4change.com, which raises money for relief agencies working to help refugees stranded around the Mediterranean, through running comedy nights at universities in the UK.

In 2016 she volunteered with an organisation working with refugees stranded on the beaches in Greece, helping them to live as best they could in such difficult and dangerous circumstances.

In that moment she realised that she needed and wanted to do something about it but wasn't too sure what to do or where to start. She knew that comedy was her passion and that, somehow, she was determined to use her skills as a comic to make a difference and Laugh 4 Change was born.

When I first met Cansu she was at the classic crossroads of direction. She had taken Laugh 4 Change as far as she thought possible and was tired and wasn't sure what to do next.

Cansu says that she never really thought about her calling as such. She's very much a reluctant superhero. She just knew that somebody had to do something and why shouldn't it be her. She said yes and took action. She started where she was – a student – used what she had – her skills as a comic and access to university rooms – and did what she could – launched a one-off comedy night asking for donations which she then sent to the NGOs working with refugees. After her first night she did another gig and then another, and is now asking herself how can she make this become a global thing.

Jo Bryant is Chief Executive and head puppeteer at www. thehands-oncompany.co.uk, a social enterprise transforming people's lives by unlocking their confidence, creativity and communication through the use of puppets. She works with schools, NGOs and corporations. She's changing lives, one puppet at a time.

When I first met Jo in 2018, she had recently changed city following on from her husband's relocation for his work. Immediately she found that she wasn't able to effectively continue managing her work remotely. She had tried to get her business running in the new location but wasn't able to get the breakthrough that she wanted. She was at the double crossroads of performance and crisis.

I took Jo back to her roots. I took her back through her life's journey looking for all of those moments in her career where she experienced her greatest levels of joy and flow. We highlighted all of the people she loved to work with, the problems she was motivated to solve, and we identified her gifts and superpowers and began to create a purpose that excited her and reconnected her with her values.

She then began the journey of letting go of the past and building powerful intentions of the work she was meant to do. Having created the intention she began to take massive daily action that took her in the direction of those dreams and is now so busy that she's taken on new staff, bought machinery to make more puppets and is in regular conversations with people and organisations wanting to partner with her.

Jo says that she always wanted to use puppets to help transform the lives of children and young people. It wasn't something that she had to fight against as it was something that she just loved to do. The challenge for her was surrendering to her calling when the going got tough. It would have been easy to give up and go and do something else instead. When she felt like that, she just kept seeing all of those children and young people smiling and laughing when they saw the puppets and she found the strength to keep going.

Surrendering to your calling transforms you and releases you to be who you really are, enjoy the life that is available to you and do the work that you were born to do.

Note from the Author: Ordinary Superheroes Wanted

I would like to extend an invitation to you to join me and be a part of this army, a global force for good. If you have a dream or a calling that you want to make happen or believe that there is work that you are meant to do, I'd like to hear from you. I'd like to help you.

We run workshops that support ordinary superheroes to find their purpose and path, to get really clear on the work that they're meant to do and to identify the right vehicle to make that happen. Mostly it's through starting projects and ventures that create impact and pay the bills.

We have helped hundreds of people to master the art of marketing and communication, supporting them to make more money and greater impact with less stress, releasing them to show up boldly in the world, sharing their message to the people who need it and creating value for them and themselves.

We are also looking for a small number of coaches, consultants, therapists, healers and helpers who sense that part of their calling is to help other people find their calling and work to make it happen. If that's you, I'd like to extend a personal invitation to join our team and train as a certified passion and purpose facilitator. To learn how to help people reconnect their hearts and heads through discovering what it is that they really want out of life and to help them to finally let go of everything that stops them from believing that it's possible and to take action to make their dreams happen.

If that's you, please reach out to me. Email me at neil@neilprem.com and let's talk.

Whatever your dream. We are here to help you make that happen.

With love and deep respect,

Your friend and fellow ordinary superhero,

Neil

Testimonials

'Neil's coaching techniques are powerful and informative, thought-provoking and inspirational. He's not only became a trusted colleague but a friend I value highly.' Christine Nottage, third sector and homelessness advocate

'Following on from your workshop, I chose to make a major move in my life. Thanks again for inspiring me to make these changes.' Sue Walden, business development specialist

'Neil guided me to unlock the potential in my idea.' Nino Singh Judge, CEO, Flypop Ltd. (www.flypop.co.uk)

'Neil held up a mirror of unconditional acceptance and positivity to me. He believed in me and helped me to believe that my dream was possible and that I had everything I needed within me to make it happen. He encouraged me to take small steps which helped unlock that confidence. Years later I have a large team of staff, volunteers and an office and full workload.' Marina Pallares, CEO, Acting Now (www.actingnow.co.uk)

'The most stimulating and thought-provoking workshop from Neil.' Andy Gilbert, pastor

'You have no idea the difference you've brought into my life. Now I have a dream and I believe it's possible.' Dhanya Gokul, social designer and co-founder, Tan-Ta-Dan (www.tantadan.in)

'Your work and message is life-changing.' Doug Williamson, financial trainer (www.accelerate-east.co.uk)

'A year ago I worked with Neil and if you'd told me then what I'd be doing now, I'd never have believed it! I'm doing more than I ever thought possible.' Suzanne Morris, photographer and designer (www.suzannemorris.co.uk)

'Neil believed in me and kept encouraging me to laugh more and more often; to not worry about what I couldn't do but always to do what I could. He kept encouraging me to think big and start small. We're on our way!' Cansu Karabiyik, comedian, Laugh 4 Change (www.facebook.com/Laugh4Change/)

'I can't say enough about how much I admire Neil and the work that he does. I often wonder would I ever be doing as much with my life if it hadn't been for him. I'd certainly be more fearful.' Jo Bryant, chief puppeteer, The Hands-on Company (www.thehands-oncompany.co.uk)

'Neil is incredible at communicating in such a natural way. He is a born encourager, inspiring people to reach for and achieve their dreams.' Gen Loaker, divorce recovery specialist (www.mosaiclives.com)

'Neil's story is deeply moving.' Simon Hall, writer and broadcaster (www.thetvdetective.com)

'Neil helped me to realise that I'm not alone in my struggles. His information and strategies are powerful.' Ian Francis, co-founder of The Sleep Lovers (www.thesleeplovers.com)

'Neil is that rare non-judgemental person who can create environments and space for learning in which I feel aligned allowing me to feel energised and think differently.' Shari Khan, trainer, leadership mentor and executive coach (www.trainsform.co.uk)

'Since meeting you Neil, I have to say it's allowed me to take a whole different look at my life and work and I can't thank you enough, I now have a fresh perspective. Whatever it is that you do, it is a talent!' Lyndsey Latarche, pre-owned furniture specialist, All Small Things

'Neil repeatedly challenged my preconceived thoughts and gave me the courage to create the vision for something which I hope will change the lives of many of the world's most disadvantaged youth for years to come.' Adriana Poglia, CEO of Peace Child International (www.peacechild.org)

'Thanks a million Neil – I really enjoyed your workshop and got a lot out of it.' Nick Askew, CEO and founder, Conservation Careers (www.conservation-careers.com)

'I met Neil for a one-to-one session where we discussed my ambitions and goals. Afterwards I had a much clearer understanding of who I am and my abilities and what exactly I want to achieve in life. If anyone has a few spare hours I would definitely recommend talking to Neil!' Pascal Loose, design engineer (@loosepascal)

'Neil was encouraging and aspirational and gave me the skills to make my business a success.' Ann Higgs, independent consultant, positive health (www.healthandwellbeingwithannhiggs.uk)

'Neil was an astute and supportive mentor, rightly divining my hopes and helping me to turn them into achievable goals. I now have every confidence to enter into the marketplace in my chosen field. As an older member of society I found him to be patient with my lack of current technological and business know-how and he inspired a sense of self-worth in me.' Margaret Coles, therapist (www.movingtherapy.co.uk)

'Neil helped me to understand what I really want and identify the first steps to work towards achieving my dreams! I am immensely grateful to Neil for providing superb clarity where confusion and mist reigned! Now I know where I am headed thanks to Neil's support!' Adelina Chalmers, communication genius (www.geekwhisperer.co.uk)

'Neil is warm and encouraging, he took us through a series of coaching sessions at our speed and with our goals in mind. He is thoughtful and generous with his time and we appreciate and value his support.' Maria Varallo, co-founder, Illuminate (www.illuminatecharity.org.uk)

'The encouragement and belief that Neil has shown me have been extremely valuable in giving me the confidence in my strengths and abilities, key to propelling me in a more focused and efficient direction.' Michelle Brace, creative producer and artist (www.collusion.org.uk)

Printed in Poland
by Amazon Fulfillment
Poland Sp. z o.o., Wrocław